THE KINGFISHER DINOSAUR ENCYCLOPEDIA

Professor Mike Benton

KINGFISHER

First published 2009 by Kingfisher
This edition published 2017 by Kingfisher
an imprint of Macmillan Children's Books
20 New Wharf Road, London N1 9RR
Associated companies throughout the world
www.panmacmillan.com

Cover design by Matthew Kelly

ISBN 978-0-7534-4149-7

1 3 5 7 9 8 6 4 2
1TR/0217/UTD/WKT/128MA

A CIP catalogue record for this book is available from the British Library.

Printed in China

Contents

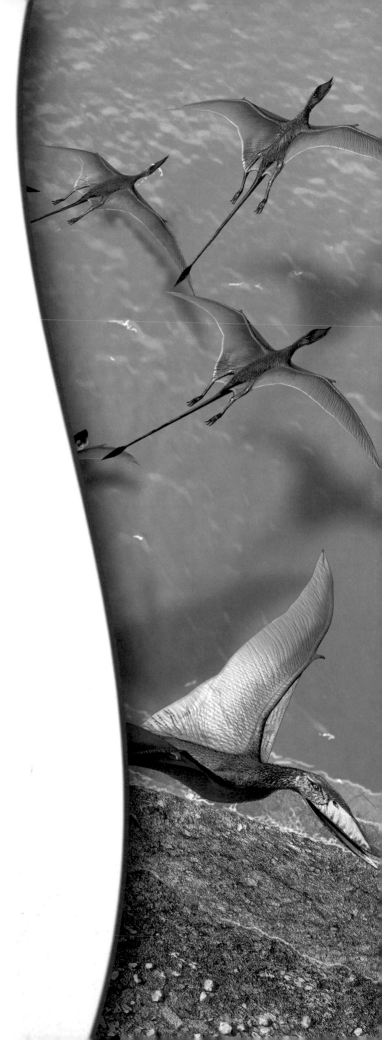

THE FIRST DINOSAURS

The first dinosaurs were small, human-sized animals that ran about on their hind legs and fed on lizard-like animals and insects. These dinosaurs were very different from the later and much larger creatures. The first dinosaurs evolved in a world that was already populated by other primitive animals, and their initial spread was the result of some lucky chances.

The prehistoric scene

Earth was already thousands of millions of years old when the dinosaurs appeared. These creatures lived a long time ago, but they were not the first forms of life on Earth.

The first dinosaurs appeared on the Earth in the Late Triassic, about 230 million years ago. Shortly before that, some small, two-legged hunting reptiles – the closest ancestors of dinosaurs yet found – lived in South America.

Marasuchus

The first fossils of the pre-dinosaur *Marasuchus* were found more than 50 years ago, but whole skeletons have been discovered since. *Marasuchus* was tiny – only 40cm long – and had needle-sharp teeth. It was an active hunter that chased small, lizard-like animals.

Lagerpeton

Lagerpeton was about the size of a chicken, but much thinner. These little reptiles were close relatives of dinosaurs. They had long, slender legs and stood high on their toes, like a modern bird. Their legs were also tucked closely under their bodies.

Dinodontosaurus

This huge reptile had sharp, bony jaws and a pair of teeth that it used to rake in plants and chop them up. At the front of the snout was a horny beak that helped cut up the tough plants. *Dinodontosaurus* was large and round because its food was of poor quality, and it needed a huge gut in order to digest everything.

A strong skeleton

This skeleton of a *Dinodontosaurus* shows its massive arms and legs. They were built like pillars to support a body that may have weighed a tonne or more. The limbs stick out at the sides a little, so *Dinodontosaurus* was probably not able to move very quickly.

Triassic palaeontology

Alfred Romer (1894–1973) was a great American palaeontologist (fossil expert) who discovered many of the remarkable Triassic beasts of South America. During expeditions in the 1950s, he and his team found up to 20 new species.

Massetognathus

In the Triassic, not only did the dinosaurs appear, but also the mammals. Although it was a reptile, *Massetognathus* is one of our distant ancestors. It had three different types of teeth – incisors, canines and grinding – as we do. Reptiles typically have only one kind of tooth.

Valley of dinosaurs

The Ischigualasto Valley in northern Argentina is key to an understanding of the very first dinosaurs. It is very hot and dry, but a fossil-hunter's paradise!

The first fossils were found in the 1950s. There have been many expeditions since then and remarkable fossils of the first dinosaurs have been unearthed.

Fossil finds

It takes many hours in the burning heat to dig out fossil bones. The bones are fragile and usually scattered, and the rock is hard. Palaeontologists have to chip away carefully, protecting the bones with glue and plaster so that they can be carried back to the laboratory.

On the surface

A collection of bones is laid out on a cloth before being individually packed up to go to a museum. Excavations have taken place in the valley since the 1920s, and over the past fifty years many thousands of bones have been dug out. The area is now a World Heritage site.

The Ischigualasto Formation

The sandstones of the Ischigualasto Valley are called the Ischigualasto Formation. Some ash beds, just below the fossil layer, have enabled experts to date the rock sequence at 228 million years old. The ash beds were formed after a nearby volcano erupted.

THE FIRST DINOSAUR

THE FIRST ANIMAL TO HAVE MOST OF THE CHARACTERISTICS OF A DINOSAUR IS *HERRERASAURUS*, FROM THE ISCHIGUALASTO FORMATION IN ARGENTINA. SEVERAL SKELETONS HAVE BEEN FOUND OF THIS 3M-LONG MEAT-EATER.

Between the eye socket and the nostril is a mystery hole, typical of all dinosaurs and their relatives. This might have housed a salt gland, or may have been there to make the skull lighter.

Hunting dinosaurs simply tore up their food and swallowed it whole. The flesh of the prey was ground up in the stomach, and the bones were partly dissolved with stomach acids.

ACTIVE HUNTERS

Herrerasaurus was a fast-moving hunter. It fed on the small reptiles of Ischigualasto times, some of them about the size of lizards or rabbits. *Herrerasaurus* probably ran faster than its prey, and it would have grabbed them in its powerful jaws or with its long, bony fingers.

HIPS AND HINDLIMBS

Although *Herrerasaurus* was much larger than *Marasuchus*, and both animals look very similar, we know that *Herrerasaurus* was a dinosaur because of its hip bones. The socket for the thigh bone was deep and there was a small hole through the hip bones. Only dinosaurs have this hole – *Marasuchus* skeletons do not have one.

Marasuchus, a close relative of the dinosaurs

Herrerasaurus, one of the first dinosaurs

INSIDE THE HEAD

The skull of *Herrerasaurus* has several openings. The pair of holes at the front of the snout are for the nostrils. At the very back are two openings, one above the other, for the jaw muscles. These muscles ran from the cheek area down to the lower jaw and they gave *Herrerasaurus* a bite powerful enough to chop off a finger. In front is the round eye socket.

The Ischigualasto Formation

Many palaeontologists have searched these rocks in Argentina for fossils of dinosaurs and other animals.

Only one or two skeletons of the Ischigualasto dinosaurs, *Herrerasaurus* and *Eoraptor*, have been found. There are many skeletons of other animals.

The 'dawn hunter'

Eoraptor means 'dawn hunter', and this small animal, about 1m long, ran quickly through the bushes and trees chasing small, lizard-sized prey. *Eoraptor* was secretive, and may have hidden in the bushes. Its skin was probably patterned to break up its outline and act as camouflage.

Eoraptor's head

This skull of *Eoraptor* is a beautiful fossil and it is nearly complete. Here, a fossil preparator is carefully removing the last pieces of rock from the ancient bones.

Eoraptor was about the size of an eight-year-old child.

Hyperodapedon

One of the most common reptiles in this area was *Hyperodapedon*, a rhynchosaur. The rhynchosaurs were plant-eaters that had massive jaws and great pavements of teeth for tearing up tough ferns and other plants. *Hyperodapedon* had a hooked snout, possibly for raking up plant roots and leaves.

Plant fossils

The rhynchosaurs and dicynodonts fed on ferns and seed ferns which were common in Ischigualasto times. Soon after, climates became drier, and these plants disappeared from much of the world.

Fossil *Dicroidium* (above) and the tree itself (right)

Pisanosaurus

Some dinosaur fossils from this area are still a mystery. Only a few bones of the plant-eater *Pisanosaurus* are known. It is probably an ornithischian dinosaur (see pp.26–7), and an ancestor of *Iguanodon*.

Ischigualastia

The other major plant-eaters of the time were the dicynodonts, great hippo-sized animals that included *Ischigualastia* and *Dinodontosaurus* (see p.11). These large reptiles moved slowly through the bushes, pulling down leaves and fronds, too big to worry about attacks from dinosaurs.

HISTORICAL DATA

NAMING DINOSAURS

When the first dinosaurs were found, nobody knew what they were – some thought the bones came from giant lizards, others said they were crocodiles. Richard Owen (1804–92), examining all the fossils in 1841, realized that they came from an extinct group. He invented the name 'dinosaur', which means 'fearfully great reptile'. Later, in 1881, he campaigned for the Natural History Museum (above) in London to be built to house natural specimens – including dinosaur fossils.

A changing world

During the Triassic, more than 200 million years ago, the world was a very different place. It was the world of the first dinosaurs.

The Triassic plant-eaters had to cope with tough plant matter, and they had to work hard to find a nourishing meal. As climates became drier, the plants changed, and major plant-eating reptiles died out.

Extinction

There were two extinctions in the Late Triassic. The first one, 225 mya, saw the end of most of the plant-eaters that lived earlier. New plant-eating dinosaurs took over.

The Carnian scene

The Carnian stage (235–228 mya) in the Late Triassic, was a time of tropical rainfall. Ferns, mosses and seed ferns flourished in a world where it rained heavily for several months of the year. The plants were different south of the equator from those in the north, and plant-eating reptiles flourished all over. But this rainy time was soon to end.

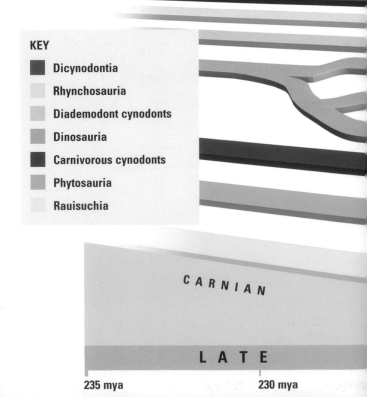

KEY

- Dicynodontia
- Rhynchosauria
- Diademodont cynodonts
- Dinosauria
- Carnivorous cynodonts
- Phytosauria
- Rauisuchia

CARNIAN

LATE

235 mya   230 mya

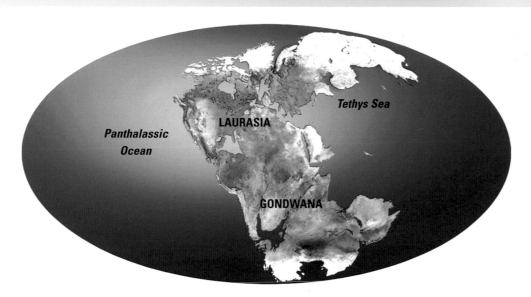

LAURASIA

Tethys Sea

Panthalassic
Ocean

GONDWANA

The world of the Carnian

During the Triassic, the continents formed a single supercontinent that stretched from the north pole to the south pole. This landmass came together as separate continents joined. It broke up slowly from the end of the Triassic.

The supercontinent was called Pangaea, and was made up of a southern continent, called Gondwana, and a northern continent, called Laurasia.

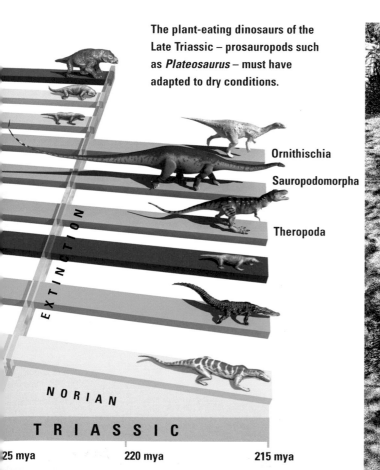

The plant-eating dinosaurs of the Late Triassic – prosauropods such as *Plateosaurus* – must have adapted to dry conditions.

Ornithischia

Sauropodomorpha

Theropoda

EXTINCTION

NORIAN

TRIASSIC

25 mya   220 mya   215 mya

The Norian scene

Conditions became drier in the Norian stage (228–203 mya) of the Late Triassic. Ferns and seed ferns died out in many areas, while conifers and other dry-loving plants spread worldwide. In many places it rained only once a year, when a torrential downpour soaked the land and sent rivers rushing furiously down ravines.

Plateosaurus

The first big dinosaurs, such as *Plateosaurus* from the Late Triassic of Germany, were plant-eaters. Great herds of the *Plateosaurus* fed on trees throughout central Europe.

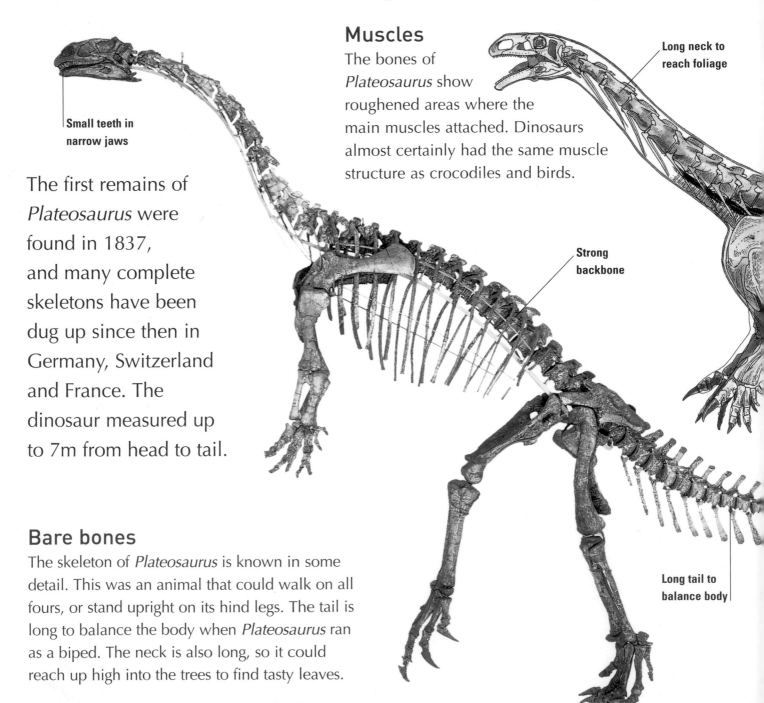

Small teeth in narrow jaws

Muscles

The bones of *Plateosaurus* show roughened areas where the main muscles attached. Dinosaurs almost certainly had the same muscle structure as crocodiles and birds.

Long neck to reach foliage

The first remains of *Plateosaurus* were found in 1837, and many complete skeletons have been dug up since then in Germany, Switzerland and France. The dinosaur measured up to 7m from head to tail.

Strong backbone

Long tail to balance body

Bare bones

The skeleton of *Plateosaurus* is known in some detail. This was an animal that could walk on all fours, or stand upright on its hind legs. The tail is long to balance the body when *Plateosaurus* ran as a biped. The neck is also long, so it could reach up high into the trees to find tasty leaves.

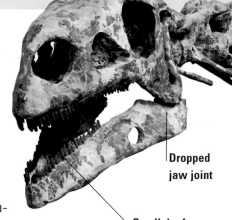

In the flesh

It is hard to add final details to a reconstruction of *Plateosaurus*. We do not know, for example, the colour of its skin. However, we do know the pattern of the skin. There are many fossils that show impressions of the scales in dinosaur skin.

Jaws and claws

Plateosaurus was one of the first plant-eating dinosaurs. Its jaws are narrow, and the jaw joint is dropped, giving a firm bite all along the jaw line. The teeth are small and not as sharp as those of flesh-eating dinosaurs. The hands, too, are modified for plant-eating. The long claws and strong fingers were used for gathering tree branches and pulling them towards the mouth.

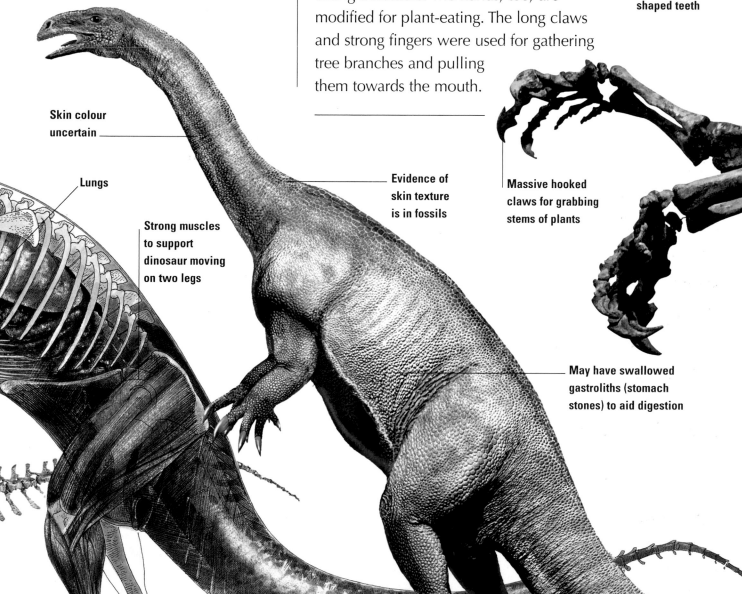

Dropped jaw joint

Small, leaf-shaped teeth

Skin colour uncertain

Lungs

Strong muscles to support dinosaur moving on two legs

Evidence of skin texture is in fossils

Massive hooked claws for grabbing stems of plants

May have swallowed gastroliths (stomach stones) to aid digestion

The Trossingen herd

The most famous *Plateosaurus* find, at Trossingen, Germany, revealed a herd of 50 or more individuals. Scientists puzzled for a long time about how they died.

Had they been trekking across a wide desert, and died from starvation and thirst? Or were they swept up in a sudden flash flood, and drowned? Modern studies of the rocks show their fossils were in sandstones from a riverbed.

First excavations

There were several major excavations at Trossingen. In the 1920s, Friedrich von Huene (1875–1969) directed huge teams of workmen, and half the hillside was dug away (above). The rock was carried away in small trucks (right) and the valuable bones taken to von Huene's university museum in nearby Tübingen.

Above: Friedrich von Huene

Right: Workers on the von Huene excavation

Modern excavation

New *Plateosaurus* remains are found from time to time. Most famous has been a huge dinosaur bone bed at Frick in Switzerland, discovered in 2007. A number of complete skeletons of *Plateosaurus* have been dug up, but it is estimated that there may be as many as another 100 skeletons to be found over the whole area.

How *Plateosaurus* moved

How did dinosaurs move? Palaeontologists can make computer models by scanning each bone, and coding the range of movements at each joint. These studies show that *Plateosaurus* walked on all fours. However, they also prove that when it ran, its arms could not cope with the fast movement, so the dinosaur's body tipped back to allow it to run on the hind legs alone.

Death in the sand

The sandstone containing the bones of the *Plateosaurus* herd is yellow and red, so von Huene thought it came from ancient desert dunes. However, modern studies show the sands were laid down by ancient rivers. A herd of the dinosaurs must have crossed a river that suddenly flooded, and dozens of panicking, thrashing dinosaurs were tumbled by the raging waters before being dumped on a sand bar downstream.

Scientists map out *Plateosaurus'* joints to create a 3D computer model that shows how the dinosaur moved.

GHOST RANCH FLOOD

ONE OF THE MOST SPECTACULAR DINOSAUR BONE
BEDS WAS FOUND AT GHOST RANCH, NEW MEXICO,
IN 1947. MORE THAN 100 SKELETONS OF THE SMALL
FLESH-EATER *COELOPHYSIS* WERE DUG UP.

A herd of *Coelophysis* head
down to the river, to drink or
to cross to the other side.

LIVING IN A HERD

These *Coelophysis* were caught up in a flood and dumped
on a sand bar. They must have been moving in a large group,
because there are very few other animals in the huge collection
of fossils. This is unusual for a predator – today, most hunting
animals either live alone or in small family groups.

FOSSIL FINDS

Most of the *Coelophysis* skeletons
(below) are complete and intact. Males
and females can be distinguished, and
even babies. One famous specimen
was thought to have been a cannibal
with a baby *Coelophysis* in its
stomach. A 2006 study showed the
'baby' was in fact a small crocodile.

EDWIN COLBERT

Edwin H Colbert (1905–2001), shown in this photograph (far right), was one of the most famous American dinosaur palaeontologists. He began his career by studying fossil mammals at the American Museum of Natural History in New York City, USA. After excavating the Ghost Ranch site in 1947, Colbert switched to studying dinosaurs and later wrote many popular books about dinosaurs and continental drift.

DINOSAUR RELATIONSHIPS

THIS REPRESENTATION OF THE DINOSAUR TREE OF LIFE SHOWS US HOW GROUPS RELATE, AND WHEN EACH GROUP CAME ON THE SCENE. PALAEONTOLOGISTS HAVE WORKED OUT THE TREE OF LIFE FOR ALL 550 DINOSAUR SPECIES.

Tyrannosaurus rex

Diplodocus

THEROPODS

SAUROPODS

Iguanodon

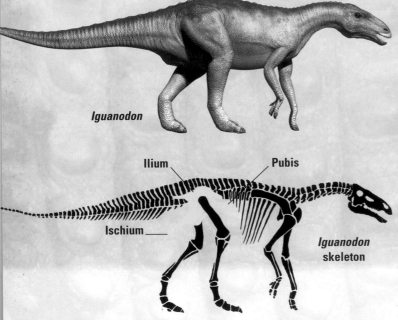

Ilium

Pubis

Ischium

Iguanodon skeleton

SAURISCHIANS

Marasuchus

SAURISCHIAN PELVIC STRUCTURE

The Dinosauria falls into two halves, the Saurischians and the Ornithischians. This was noted by palaeontologist Harry Seeley in 1887. Saurischians, including the flesh-eating theropods and the long-necked plant-eating sauropodomorphs, have a set of hip bones that point in three directions – the pubis points forwards, the ischium backwards and the ilium is on top. This is the arrangement of bones found in other reptiles, such as crocodiles, lizards and turtles, and is said to be the 'primitive' reptilian arrangement.

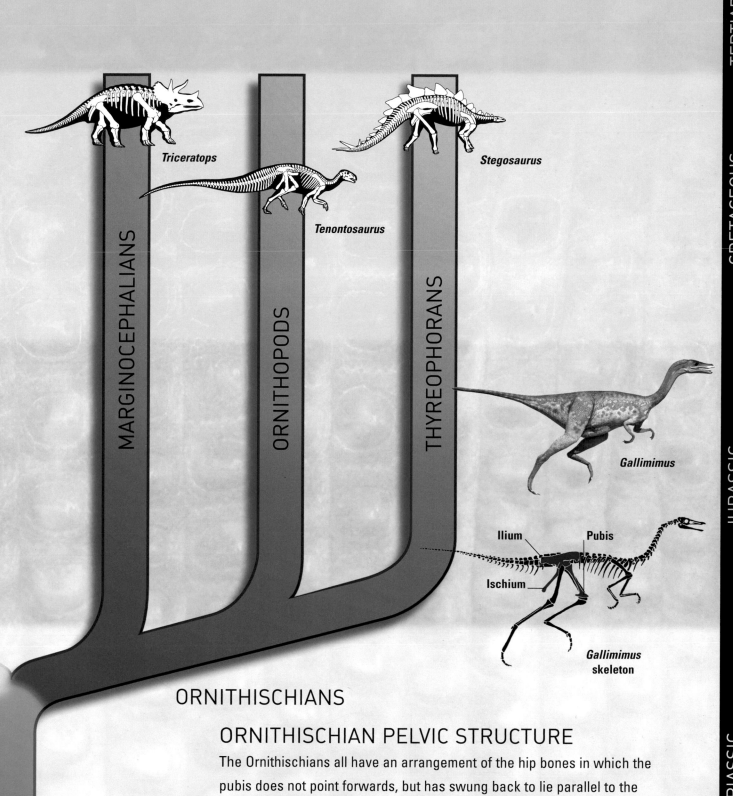

Triceratops

Tenontosaurus

Stegosaurus

MARGINOCEPHALIANS

ORNITHOPODS

THYREOPHORANS

Gallimimus

Ilium

Pubis

Ischium

Gallimimus skeleton

TERTIARY

CRETACEOUS

JURASSIC

TRIASSIC

ORNITHISCHIANS

ORNITHISCHIAN PELVIC STRUCTURE

The Ornithischians all have an arrangement of the hip bones in which the pubis does not point forwards, but has swung back to lie parallel to the ischium. The Ornithischians and Saurischians split apart in the Late Triassic, some 230 mya. Ornithischians include the Marginocephalians (with horns and thickened skulls), the Ornithopods (two-legged plant-eaters without armour) and the Thyreophorans (armoured ankylosaurs and stegosaurs).

The Bristol caves

Some amazing early fossils of the Late Triassic come from ancient caves in southwest England, UK.

The animals lived on an upland limestone pavement that had been cracked by rainwater. Centuries of rain had created many cracks, ravines and caves in the limestone landscape.

Thecodontosaurus

The dinosaur found near Bristol is *Thecodontosaurus*, one of the first plant-eating dinosaurs. It was a small animal that walked on its hind legs, using its arms to gather plants. Its teeth were small and delicate, adapted for slicing plant stems and leaves.

The Bristol fauna

Side by side with the dinosaur *Thecodontosaurus* (top) lived a whole range of lizard-like animals, one of them called *Clevosaurus* (above). These are not true lizards, but relatives of the tuatara, a 'living fossil' from New Zealand that is very like its Triassic ancestors.

Kuehneosaurus was about 70cm long, and its 'wings' were 14cm across.

Kuehneosaurus

One of the most extraordinary Bristol creatures from the Late Triassic was a gliding animal. *Kuehneosaurus* had long ribs that stuck out at the side and were almost certainly covered with skin. It could leap and glide from tree to tree.

Fossil finds

The first fossils of the Bristol beasts – bones of *Thecodontosaurus* – were found in 1834. They were in a limestone quarry in the city. Since then, hundreds of bones and skeletons have been excavated, but they all belong to quite small animals – small enough to fall into the cracks and caves!

Revealed in the rocks

As the quarrymen work through the great walls of limestone, they sometimes spot a reddish streak (right). The red rock is sand or mud filling an ancient cave system. This contains plants and – rarely – insects. Quite often there are the bones of small creatures – *Clevosaurus* and its relatives, and the gliding *Kuehneosaurus*. Palaeontologists have to sieve the sediment and pick out the delicate bones very carefully, sometimes using a dental drill.

Dinosaurs take over

Dinosaur numbers grew after two extinctions. The first, at the end of the Carnian, wiped out plant-eaters.

The second, at the end of the Triassic, caused many meat-eaters to disappear. New groups of dinosaurs flourished and took their place.

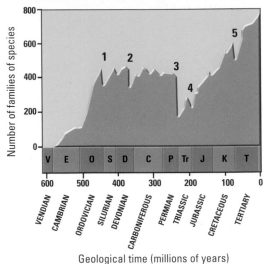

Geological time (millions of years)

The end-Triassic mass extinction

This happened 200 million years ago, and it did not just affect reptiles and dinosaurs on land. It was also a time when many groups of shellfish and fishes in the sea, as well as land plants and other animals, disappeared. Explanations have included the impact of a giant meteorite, and global warming.

The five extinctions

Five times, life on Earth has nearly disappeared. The fourth was at the end of the Triassic. The most famous of these 'big five' was the fifth, at the end of the Cretaceous, when the dinosaurs finally became extinct.

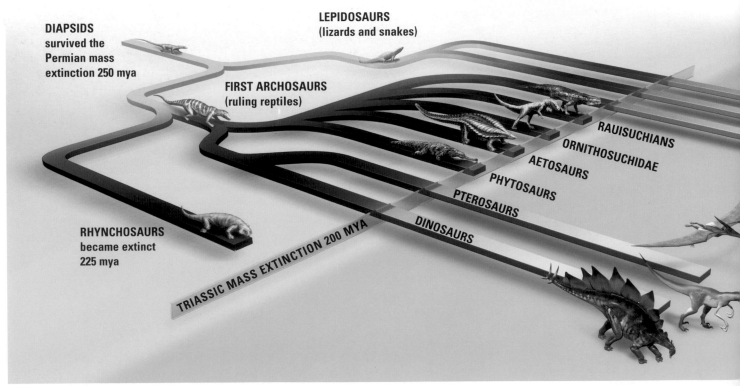

DIAPSIDS survived the Permian mass extinction 250 mya

LEPIDOSAURS (lizards and snakes)

FIRST ARCHOSAURS (ruling reptiles)

RAUISUCHIANS

ORNITHOSUCHIDAE

AETOSAURS

PHYTOSAURS

PTEROSAURS

DINOSAURS

TRIASSIC MASS EXTINCTION 200 MYA

RHYNCHOSAURS became extinct 225 mya

A new boundary

The boundary between the Triassic and Jurassic can be seen in many parts of the world. In Europe, this was a time of change, when red rocks were deposited in hot deserts, and lakes and rivers gave way to marine rocks. There was a great flooding of the sea over Europe, and in places the switch from red desert rocks to black marine rocks is clear.

The Manicouagan crater

There was great excitement in the 1980s when a huge crater, about 100km wide, was identified in Canada. It was only when scientists saw the first satellite photographs that they could see the very clear circular outline, now filled with rivers and lakes. The crater was first dated at the Triassic–Jurassic boundary, but we now know that it is much older, at 215 million years.

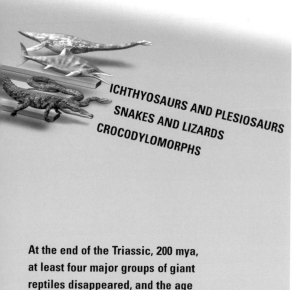

ICHTHYOSAURS AND PLESIOSAURS
SNAKES AND LIZARDS
CROCODYLOMORPHS

At the end of the Triassic, 200 mya, at least four major groups of giant reptiles disappeared, and the age of the dinosaurs began.

Global warming

There were major volcanic eruptions on the site of the North Atlantic as the great ocean began to open up. Europe was joined to North America, until massive splits in the Earth's crust began to appear. These rifts were driven by volcanic eruptions that sent clouds of gas into the atmosphere. There was a time of global warming and life in the sea stagnated. Many species died out.

Dinosaur facts

The Triassic Period began and ended with a mass extinction, a time when half or more of the species on Earth disappeared. The end of the dinosaurs, 65 mya, was another mass extinction. These were three of five such crises for life on Earth.

THE FIVE GREAT EXTINCTIONS

This diagram (right) shows the way life has expanded through time. The first life in the sea arose 3,500 mya, deep in the Precambrian era. Then sea creatures became more common and larger at the beginning of the Palaeozoic era, 540 mya. Plants and insects moved onto land about 450 mya, followed by the first amphibians 400 mya. The first two mass extinctions had major effects on life in the sea. Then, at the end of the Palaeozoic came the biggest crisis of all. The fourth and fifth mass extinctions ended the Triassic (see pp.30–1) and the Cretaceous (see pp.150–1).

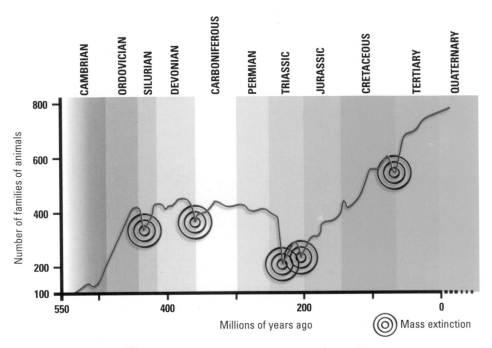

CAMBRIAN · ORDOVICIAN · SILURIAN · DEVONIAN · CARBONIFEROUS · PERMIAN · TRIASSIC · JURASSIC · CRETACEOUS · TERTIARY · QUATERNARY

Number of families of animals

800 · 600 · 400 · 200 · 100

550 · 400 · 200 · 0

Millions of years ago   ◎ Mass extinction

A *Coelophysis* fossil, with its last meal – a crocodile ancestor – in its stomach, found at Ghost Ranch in 1947

WEBSITES ON GEOLOGICAL TIME AND MASS EXTINCTIONS

www.ucmp.berkeley.edu/exhibits/index.php   A guide to the history of life.

www.cotf.edu/ete/modules/msese/earthsysflr/geotime.html   Work your way through time.

www.fossilmuseum.net/GeologicalTimeMachine.htm   The geological timescale.

www.pbs.org/wgbh/nova/evolution/brief-history-life.html   The history of life on Earth.

A WORLD OF DINOSAURS

Even after the dinosaur predators had been wiped out by the mass extinction at the end of the Triassic, it took the dinosaurs much of the next 30 million years to grow really large. The Early Jurassic began with Triassic-style dinosaurs. New forms, such as armoured dinosaurs and large predators, only came on the scene during the Middle Jurassic.

Dinosaurs of South Africa

The Jurassic period (200 to 145 million years ago) began very differently from the Triassic. New dinosaur groups came on the scene, most notably the plant-eating ornithopods.

The first ornithopods – bird-hipped dinosaurs that ran on two legs – are known from the Elliott Formation and the Clarens Formation of South Africa. These rock formations have been studied for 150 years, and continue to produce remarkable finds.

Lesothosaurus

One of the best known of the Early Jurassic ornithopods, *Lesothosaurus* was a small animal about the size of a 12-year-old child. It had long powerful legs for running fast, and quite small arms. But its plant-eating habits are given away by its jaws and teeth. The jaws are designed to give a long, firm bite all along their length, from front to back, and the teeth are small and peg-like.

The skull has a large eye socket, and a special pointed bone to support the eyeball. It is not known why ornithopods had this special bone, because their eyes were not especially large when compared to other dinosaurs.

Eye socket with pointed bone

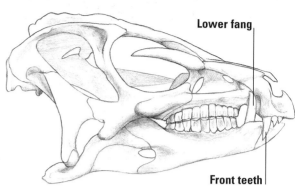

Lower fang

The lower fang was so huge there is a deep pit in the side of the snout for it.

The front teeth were good at snipping off leaves.

Front teeth

Heterodontosaurus

A relative of *Lesothosaurus*, *Heterodontosaurus* had the most amazing teeth of any dinosaur. Its pointed front teeth were perfect for cutting leaves from plants. The long canines and broad grinding teeth behind chopped up the food. The sharp fangs may even have been used as weapons for fighting.

Massospondylus

This giant plant-eating dinosaur was a relative of *Plateosaurus* (see pp.20–1). At 4–6m long, it may have weighed more than two tonnes. It is also known from North America, proving that these early dinosaurs could wander anywhere over the supercontinent Pangaea.

The long neck was useful for reaching high into trees.

The tiny teeth were used for cutting leaves but not for chewing.

The Kayenta Formation

In Arizona, in the southwestern USA, there is an area famous for fossils of Early Jurassic dinosaurs.

The rocks were laid down in hot, dry conditions. They preserved hundreds of skeletons of dinosaurs, crocodiles, mammals and other creatures.

The Kayenta outcrop

The Kayenta Formation is up to 100m thick in some places, and it is made up of layers of red, orange and yellow sandstones and mudstones. Comparison with modern deserts allows geologists to identify just how the ancient sandstones were laid down.

Sand dune features

Some of the Kayenta sandstones were laid down in deserts, and others in rivers and lakes. The ancient desert sands still show the great sweeping layers of ancient dunes. The rounded sand grains of today first tumbled and blew across these wild plains nearly 200 million years ago.

The badlands

Today, the Kayenta Formation is located in a large desert in northern Arizona. In the modern Arizona desert, the rocks often stand up as wild bluffs and pinnacles, a backdrop to many cowboy films! Modern winds have shaped the rocks. Rare torrential rain swells the streams in the ravines, and these hurtle across the countryside, cutting great gashes, and removing soil and plants. Normally, only cactuses and sagebrush can grow in such dry conditions.

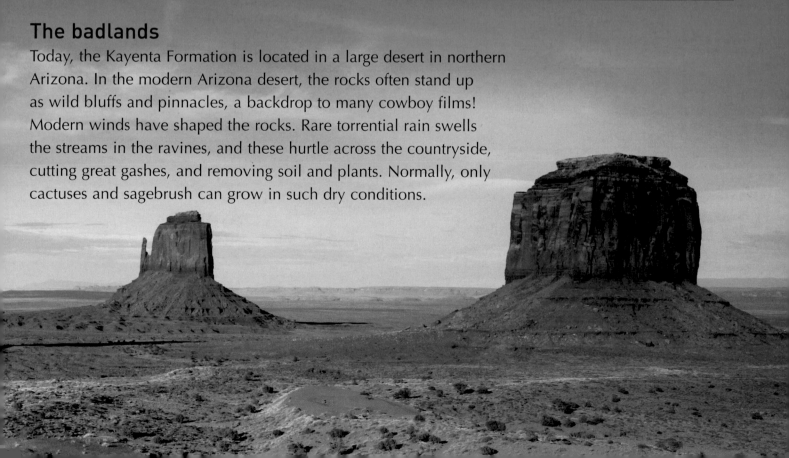

Kayenta dinosaurs

Dinosaurs from the Kayenta include the first truly large meat-eaters, and animals found on other continents.

Most of the Kayenta dinosaurs and crocodiles had close relatives in South Africa, and even in China, where *Dilophosaurus* was found in 1987.

Dilophosaurus footprint

It is not often that footprints can be matched exactly to a dinosaur. However, prints of a large theropod were found just a few metres below the skeletons of the two *Dilophosaurus*.

The long teeth even extended below the jaw line when the mouth was shut.

Syntarsus

A fossil of *Syntarsus*, a small, flesh-eating dinosaur, was found in South Africa in 1969. A well-preserved skull was found in Arizona, USA, in 1989. Such a migration, although debated, was possible because there was only one supercontinent, Pangaea.

Dilophosaurus

The most amazing dinosaur from the Kayenta Formation is *Dilophosaurus*, excavated in 1942, and first identified as *Megalosaurus*, a dinosaur already known from the Middle Jurassic of England (see pp.56–7). Then another skeleton was found, which showed the head crests – two thin bone ridges that run the length of the skull. Their function is uncertain. They were probably used for signalling 'Look out!' or 'I'm looking for a mate' to other *Dilophosaurus*.

Protosuchus

Crocodiles arose during the Triassic, and in the Jurassic some became sea-dwellers (see p.90), while others took to the land. *Protosuchus* was only 1m long, but was armed with bony plates down its back. It had powerful jaws, and may have fed on fish or small land animals.

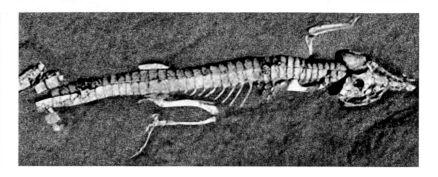

A crocodile skeleton

The first skeleton of *Protosuchus* was found in 1931 by the great fossil collector Barnum Brown, and it is now in the American Museum of Natural History in New York. It had a long snout (above right), as well as a remarkable double row of armour plates that ran along the middle of the back. The back legs were quite long, but *Protosuchus* probably ran about on all fours like a modern crocodile.

Camp and Welles

Many of the Kayenta beasts were collected and studied by two great palaeontologists from the University of California at Berkeley, Charles Camp (1893–1975) and Sam Welles (1909–97). Camp worked on many different fossil groups, from lizards to dinosaurs, and taught Sam Welles.

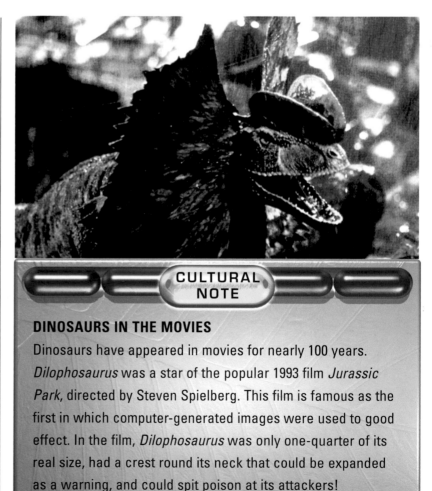

CULTURAL NOTE

DINOSAURS IN THE MOVIES

Dinosaurs have appeared in movies for nearly 100 years. *Dilophosaurus* was a star of the popular 1993 film *Jurassic Park*, directed by Steven Spielberg. This film is famous as the first in which computer-generated images were used to good effect. In the film, *Dilophosaurus* was only one-quarter of its real size, had a crest round its neck that could be expanded as a warning, and could spit poison at its attackers!

Dinosaur footprints

The Kayenta Formation is one of the places famous for dinosaur footprints as well as skeletons. The footprints tell us a great deal about how dinosaurs lived.

For one thing, a track of prints tells us that a particular dinosaur walked across this spot on a particular day. Footprints actually show us scenes from dinosaur life!

MAKING FOOTPRINTS

Dinosaur footprints give clues about the animal that made them. These fossils provide invaluable information for palaeontologists.

The dinosaur steps on soft mud and sand, leaving an impression.

The footprint impression fills up with more sand or mud.

Over a period of millions of years, the mud gradually turns to rock.

The material filling the impression washes out, leaving a rocky footprint.

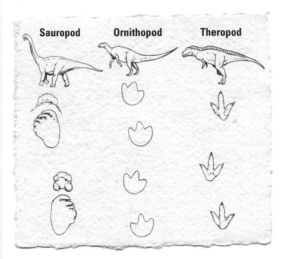

Sauropod   Ornithopod   Theropod

Track types

Dinosaur footprints can be identified, to major groups at least. They vary enormously in size from little prints, the size of a turkey's foot, to massive prints several metres across made by sauropods. Different dinosaurs had different numbers of toes, and the footprints can even show whether a dinosaur had claws or hooves.

Calculating speed

If an animal walks, its footprints are close together. If it runs fast, they are far apart. If you know the height of the animal that made a set of tracks, you can calculate how fast it was moving. If you know the leg length, you can calculate the length of the strides.

0
km/h 7   27   43.4   88.6 101.4

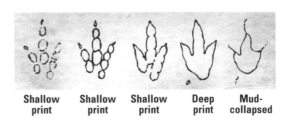

Shallow   Shallow   Shallow   Deep   Mud-
print   print   print   print   collapsed

Interpreting tracks

Tracks show many other things apart from what made the prints and how fast they were moving. Some show herds of dinosaurs, sometimes even with young protected in the middle of the herd. Others show where a herd of plant-eaters have scattered in front of a marauding predator!

A dinosaur trail

This remarkable track from the Late Cretaceous of the Canadian Rocky Mountains shows where an ankylosaur took a walk 70 million years ago. There are two rows of prints, from the left- and right-hand sides of the animal, and each print is a pair – the print of the hand and then the foot. Each print is a metre or so apart, so this track was made by an ankylosaur, such as *Ankylosaurus*, walking quite slowly.

Dinosaurs of Lufeng

China is famous for its dinosaurs, and some of the first to be discovered in that country were the Lufeng dinosaurs, unearthed in the 1930s.

EVOLUTION

These skulls show the gradual change in skull shape from early reptiles to the first mammals of the Late Triassic and Early Jurassic.

Reptiles have a jaw joint right at the back and many bones in the lower jaw.

The mammal-like reptiles of the Triassic had a shorter lower jaw with fewer bones.

The first mammals had a different jaw joint and only one bone in the lower jaw.

The Lufeng rocks are Early Jurassic in age, the same as the Kayenta Formation, and the dinosaurs are similar. However, the species are different. Most of them are large plant-eaters, with a few smaller forms and some early mammals.

Lufengosaurus

Hundreds of skeletons have been dug up since *Lufengosaurus* was first found. There are bones of males, females and juveniles. These animals roamed in huge herds, stripping trees and bushes of all their leaves. They could rear up on their hind legs, stretching up to 4m to reach the highest branches. Their large hands, with massive thumb claws, may have been used for gathering leaves or perhaps for self-defence.

Tiny head

Long neck

Long tail

Yunnanosaurus

Fossils of *Yunnanosaurus*, a close relative of *Lufengosaurus*, are much less common. It had unusual spoon-shaped teeth that suggest it was more closely related to later sauropod dinosaurs (see pp.60–1). It was also larger, at up to 7m.

Powerful hips and hind legs

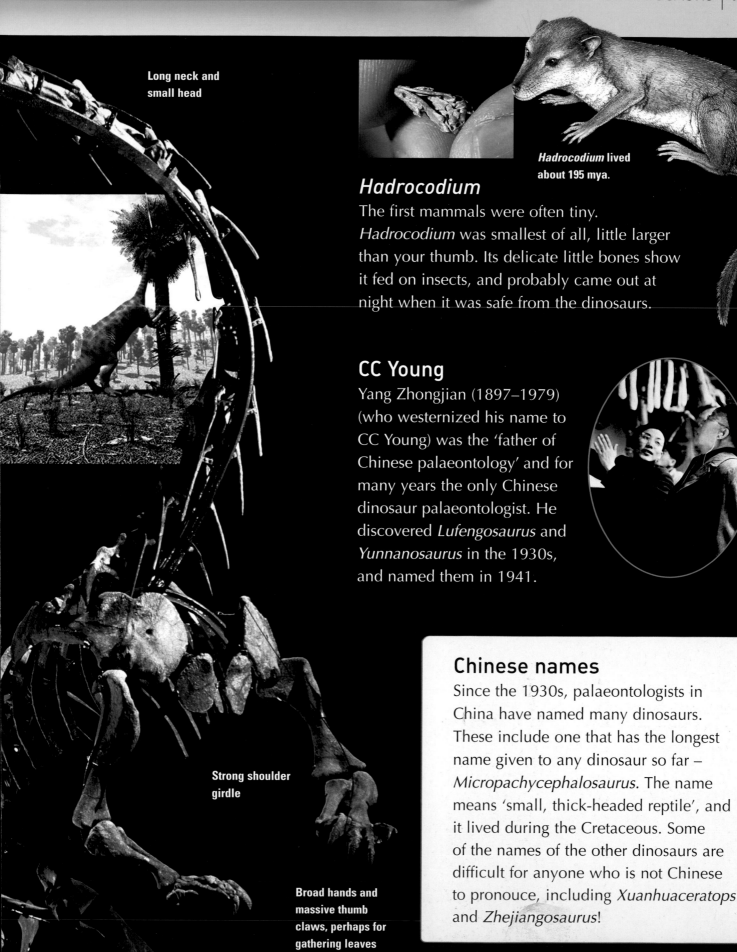

**Long neck and
small head**

Hadrocodium lived
about 195 mya.

Hadrocodium

The first mammals were often tiny.
Hadrocodium was smallest of all, little larger
than your thumb. Its delicate little bones show
it fed on insects, and probably came out at
night when it was safe from the dinosaurs.

CC Young

Yang Zhongjian (1897–1979)
(who westernized his name to
CC Young) was the 'father of
Chinese palaeontology' and for
many years the only Chinese
dinosaur palaeontologist. He
discovered *Lufengosaurus* and
Yunnanosaurus in the 1930s,
and named them in 1941.

**Strong shoulder
girdle**

**Broad hands and
massive thumb
claws, perhaps for
gathering leaves**

Chinese names

Since the 1930s, palaeontologists in
China have named many dinosaurs.
These include one that has the longest
name given to any dinosaur so far –
Micropachycephalosaurus. The name
means 'small, thick-headed reptile', and
it lived during the Cretaceous. Some
of the names of the other dinosaurs are
difficult for anyone who is not Chinese
to pronouce, including *Xuanhuaceratops*
and *Zhejiangosaurus*!

ARMOURED DINOSAURS

In the Early Jurassic the first armoured dinosaurs appeared. The armour meant that these plant-eaters probably had a better chance of surviving an attack from a big meat-eating dinosaur.

SKIN FOSSILS

This section of the skin of a *Scelidosaurus* (below) shows many small bone plates in a crazy-paving pattern, just as they would have been in life. Skeletons of *Scelidosaurus* were usually washed into the sea, and the flesh and skin lost. This one must have been buried deep in the mud before any sharks or crabs could tear off its skin and flesh.

The English lagoon of 190 mya was tropical. Small islands dotted the scene, and dinosaurs lived near the shore.

DYNAMICS OF A FOSSIL

This fossil shows the skull and neck of a *Scelidosaurus*, with large armour plates running down the back of the neck. Part of the tip of the snout was broken off when the fossil was collected, and is on a separate small block at the left. *Scelidosaurus'* quite small, leaf-shaped teeth, good for chopping ferns, are clearly visible along each jaw.

DINOSAURS OF THE SHORE

A herd of *Scelidosaurus* feed on low vegetation by the shores of the Early Jurassic sea in southern England. These were some of the first dinosaurs to walk on all fours all of the time. They were 4m long, and had short legs because they did not need to run fast. They had small armour plates in the skin, and rows of larger plates and spines.

The Lias and the Jurassic

How do we know the ages of all the dinosaurs, and date the rocks in which they are found? We find out this information from stratigraphy, the study of geological time.

Stratigraphy is the study of strata, or rock layers. Early scientists thought rocks and fossils were found randomly in different places, without any real meaning. Then, the first geologists – experts on rocks – realized that there were patterns.

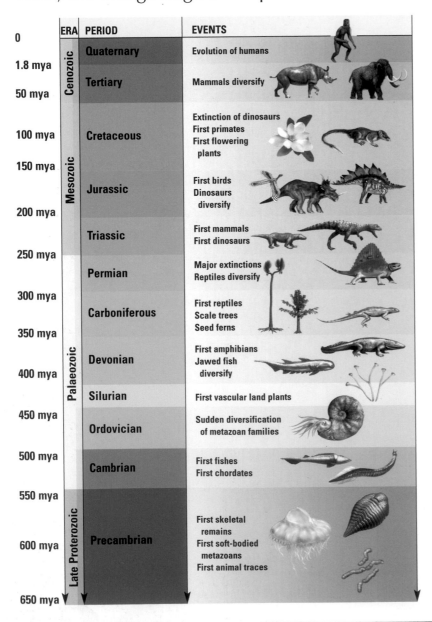

	ERA	PERIOD	EVENTS
0	Cenozoic	Quaternary	Evolution of humans
1.8 mya		Tertiary	Mammals diversify
50 mya			
100 mya	Mesozoic	Cretaceous	Extinction of dinosaurs First primates First flowering plants
150 mya		Jurassic	First birds Dinosaurs diversify
200 mya		Triassic	First mammals First dinosaurs
250 mya	Palaeozoic	Permian	Major extinctions Reptiles diversify
300 mya		Carboniferous	First reptiles Scale trees Seed ferns
350 mya		Devonian	First amphibians Jawed fish diversify
400 mya		Silurian	First vascular land plants
450 mya		Ordovician	Sudden diversification of metazoan families
500 mya		Cambrian	First fishes First chordates
550 mya	Late Proterozoic	Precambrian	First skeletal remains First soft-bodied metazoans First animal traces
600 mya			
650 mya			

A geological time scale

Younger rocks lie on top of older rocks. So, by working up and down cliffs and quarries, geologists can work out the relative ages of the rocks, from most ancient to most recent. In the 1820s and 1830s, experts began to divide up the great thicknesses of rocks into geological periods – Triassic, Jurassic, Cretaceous. Later, they were able to calculate exact dates, in millions of years, using the rate of decay of radioactive minerals.

Biostratigraphy

The key to matching rocks from place to place is the fossils. The Lias rock formation of southern England is dated as 'Early Jurassic' because of its fossils. Similar fossils have been found in France and Germany. This process of comparing and matching is known as biostratigraphy.

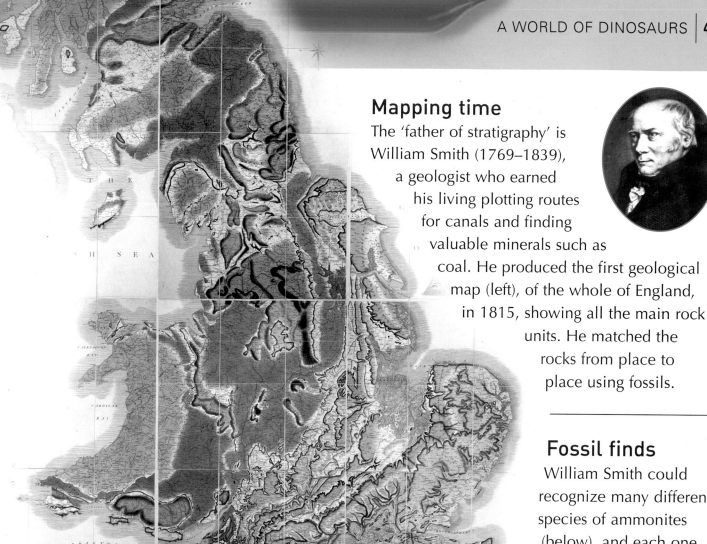

Mapping time

The 'father of stratigraphy' is William Smith (1769–1839), a geologist who earned his living plotting routes for canals and finding valuable minerals such as coal. He produced the first geological map (left), of the whole of England, in 1815, showing all the main rock units. He matched the rocks from place to place using fossils.

Fossil finds

William Smith could recognize many different species of ammonites (below), and each one marked a particular age zone in the rocks. Ammonites swam in the Jurassic seas, with bodies like squid or octopus inside a circular shell.

Fossil ammonites

The cliffs of Lyme Regis

Some of the most famous Lias fossils, including the armoured dinosaur *Scelidosaurus*, come from cliffs near the small fishing town of Lyme Regis in Dorset, southern England. The layers of limestone and mudstone were quarried for building stone. The ammonites and other fossil shellfish, as well as occasional bones, are collected by many people.

GIANTS OF THE LIAS

While some of the first dinosaurs walked on land, giant reptiles of all shapes and sizes stalked the Lias seas. They fed on ammonites, fish… and each other!

DANGEROUS WATERS

The most common reptiles in the Lias seas were the ichthyosaurs, or 'fish reptiles'. Ichthyosaurs looked like modern sharks or dolphins. They swam fast by beating their tail from side to side, and fed on belemnites and fishes, as shown by their stomach contents. The long-necked reptiles are plesiosaurs, and they swam by 'underwater flying', beating their paddles and pursuing fish and even smaller ichthyosaurs.

A coiled ammonite

The plesiosaur *Plesiosaurus*

MARY ANNING

Mary Anning (1799–1847) is one of the most famous fossil collectors. She came from a poor fishing family that lived in Lyme Regis, but she had great skill at finding fossils and cutting them out of the rock. She found the first ichthyosaur and plesiosaur fossils at Lyme Regis, as well as the first flying reptiles and many ammonites and fishes. She sold them all to museums in England.

The ichthyosaur
Ichthyosaurus

FOSSIL FINDS

Some of the fossils found in the Lyme Regis area are amazing. This ichthyosaur fossil shows every bone in place, the long pointed snout and the front paddles below the rib cage. The body must have fallen to the sea bed and been covered by black mud without undergoing any disturbance.

Dinosaurs of Antarctica

In the Mesozoic, Antarctica was not covered with ice, climates were much warmer and there were lush forests. Dinosaurs were not common because winters were cold.

The first dinosaurs from Antarctica were found only 20 years ago, and several skeletons have been excavated since. The effort needed to dig the fossils out of the icy ground is enormous!

Working in Antarctica

Expeditions cost a great deal of money. Ships, planes and helicopters are needed to carry people and all their equipment to the site. At the end of the summer, absolutely everything has to be brought home. Even the scientists' urine and other waste has to be taken away.

In the field

During the southern summer in Antarctica, the snow melts and geologists can see the rocks. During this short summer season, the scientists must complete their work as fast as they can. Even though the snow has melted, the air is still cold, and they have to wear thick clothes.

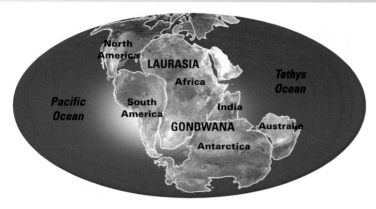

Antarctica and Africa

Today, Antarctica is a huge island that lies over the south pole. In the Triassic and Jurassic, Antarctica was connected to Africa, and it lay further north. Dinosaurs could stay there during summer, but winters were probably cold, so they may have migrated north to Africa.

Glacialisaurus

'Frozen reptile' is a good name for an Antarctic dinosaur, but this Early Jurassic animal did not live on the ice. It is known from only a few leg bones found on Mount Kirkpatrick, but these show that it was a prosauropod related to *Lufengosaurus* from China (see pp.42–3).

Cryolophosaurus

The first Antarctic dinosaur to be named was also the most spectacular. *Cryolophosaurus* was a theropod with an extraordinary bony crest on its forehead, just in front of the eyes. The crest may have been brightly coloured and used for signalling. This flesh-eater was probably related to *Dilophosaurus* (see p.38).

Tritylodontid

Other fossils from the Early Jurassic of Antarctica include fragments of a pterosaur and some other dinosaurs, as well as tree trunks and other plants. One unusual fossil is a tritylodontid (below), known from a single tooth. Tritylodontids were close relatives of mammals and they fed on tough plants that they ground up with massive teeth.

THE ORIGIN OF BIRDS

PEOPLE OFTEN SAY THAT
BIRDS ARE 'LIVING DINOSAURS',
BUT WHAT DOES THIS MEAN?
CAREFUL STUDY OF DINOSAUR
BONES ALLOWS SCIENTISTS TO
DRAW DETAILED FAMILY TREES.
IT IS CLEAR FROM THESE THAT
BIRDS ARE DINOSAURS.

ANCESTRAL LINE

Birds are theropods because they share dozens
of features in the skull, backbone, hands and feet.
Birds are coelurosaurs because they have long
arms and feathers, like all coelurosaur dinosaurs.
The skeleton of the first bird, *Archaeopteryx*, is
just like that of a small, flesh-eating dinosaur.

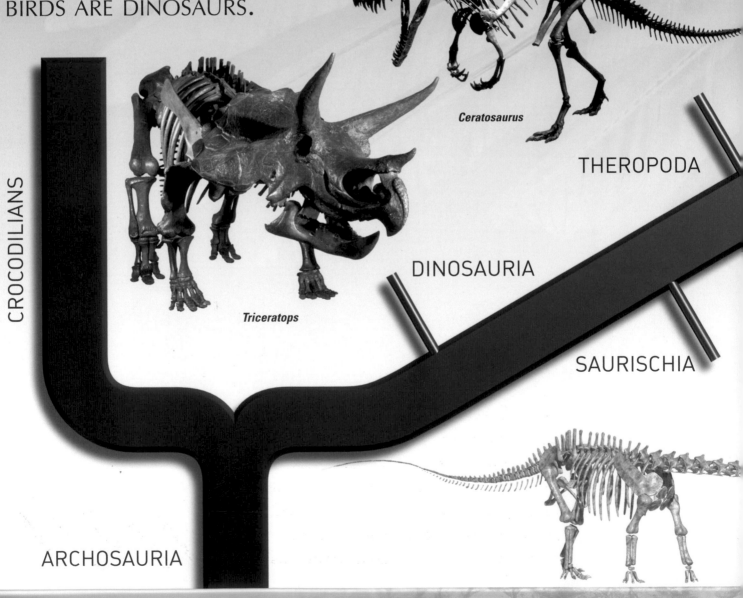

Ceratosaurus

Triceratops

CROCODILIANS

THEROPODA

DINOSAURIA

SAURISCHIA

ARCHOSAURIA

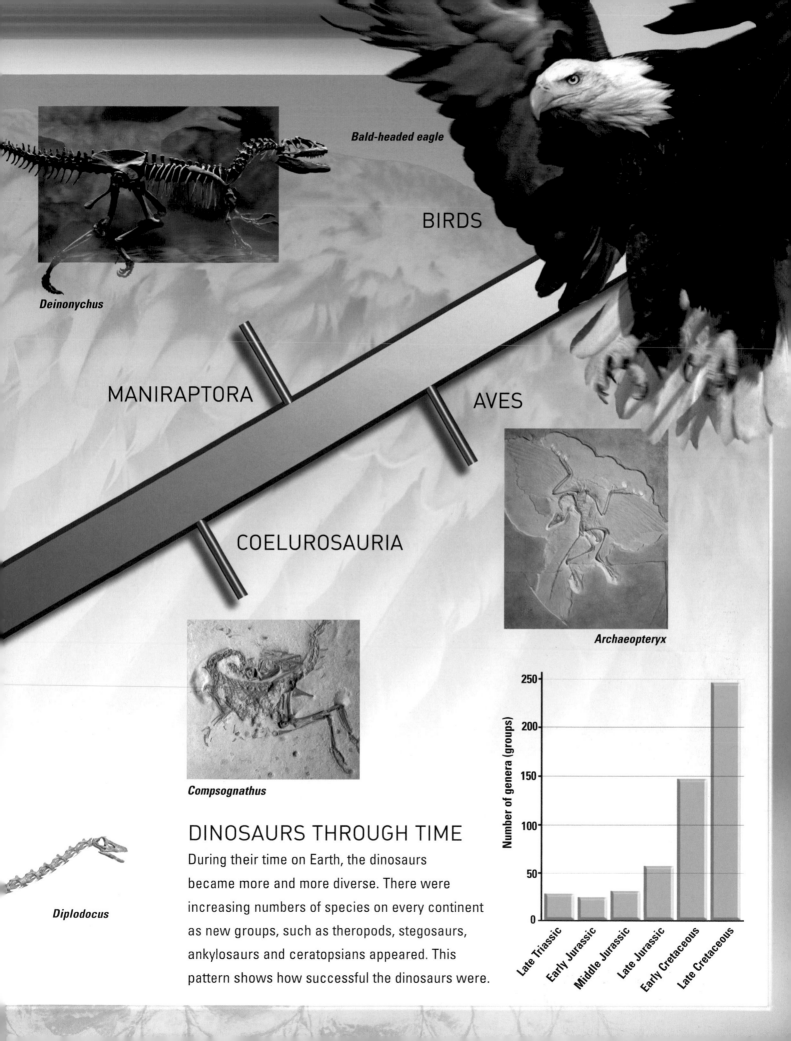

Bald-headed eagle

BIRDS

Deinonychus

MANIRAPTORA

AVES

COELUROSAURIA

Archaeopteryx

Compsognathus

Diplodocus

DINOSAURS THROUGH TIME

During their time on Earth, the dinosaurs became more and more diverse. There were increasing numbers of species on every continent as new groups, such as theropods, stegosaurs, ankylosaurs and ceratopsians appeared. This pattern shows how successful the dinosaurs were.

Number of genera (groups)

250
200
150
100
50
0

Late Triassic
Early Jurassic
Middle Jurassic
Late Jurassic
Early Cretaceous
Late Cretaceous

Theropods

The meat-eating dinosaurs, small and large, were all theropods. They had sharp teeth that curved back, and powerful jaw muscles.

Theropods appeared in the Triassic, but large theropods such as *Dilophosaurus* and *Megalosaurus* dominated in the Jurassic.

Teeth

Nearly all theropods had more or less the same kinds of teeth. The teeth were curved back, which meant that struggling prey animals could not escape! The front and back edges of the teeth were sharp and had a zig-zag edge like that of a steak knife.

Arms and legs

Theropods all ran on their hind legs, and kept their arms free. Surprisingly, most theropods probably did not use their arms for fighting with their prey. Instead, they attacked by biting the back of the prey's neck and either wrestled it to the ground, or followed it as it weakened. They then held the prey down with their foot, and tore at the flesh.

The wrong shape

The first theropod to be found, *Megalosaurus* (see pp.56–7), was known first only from a few bones. Its discoverer, William Buckland, thought it was a giant lizard, while Richard Owen thought it may be a mammal. The drawing (above) shows something that is a cross between a lion and a crocodile!

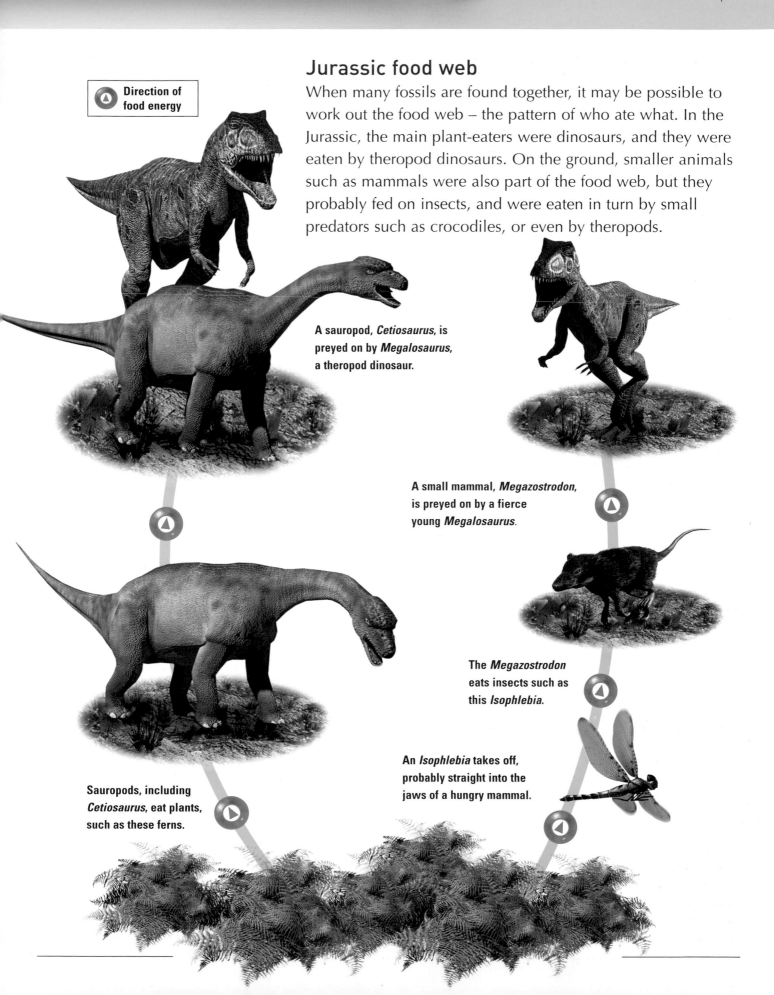

Direction of food energy

Jurassic food web

When many fossils are found together, it may be possible to work out the food web – the pattern of who ate what. In the Jurassic, the main plant-eaters were dinosaurs, and they were eaten by theropod dinosaurs. On the ground, smaller animals such as mammals were also part of the food web, but they probably fed on insects, and were eaten in turn by small predators such as crocodiles, or even by theropods.

A sauropod, *Cetiosaurus*, is preyed on by *Megalosaurus*, a theropod dinosaur.

A small mammal, *Megazostrodon*, is preyed on by a fierce young *Megalosaurus*.

The *Megazostrodon* eats insects such as this *Isophlebia*.

Sauropods, including *Cetiosaurus*, eat plants, such as these ferns.

An *Isophlebia* takes off, probably straight into the jaws of a hungry mammal.

Half the weight of a theropod such as *Megalosaurus* was in the tail. This allowed it to keep its balance as it ran on its two hind legs. The most powerful muscles of the hind leg were in the root of the tail, and the tail switched from side to side as the animal walked along.

MEGALOSAURUS

THE TERROR OF THE MIDDLE JURASSIC, *MEGALOSAURUS* WAS SOME 9M LONG AND WEIGHED ABOUT A TONNE. THIS THEROPOD HAD POWERFUL HINDLIMBS FOR FAST MOVEMENT, AND STRONG HANDS AND ARMS FOR GRASPING ITS PREY. IT WAS A RUTHLESS HUNTER OF PREY, EVEN EATING LARGE BEASTS SUCH AS SAUROPODS.

FIERCE PREDATOR

Megalosaurus is now known from the Middle Jurassic of England, France and Portugal. In each of these places, *Megalosaurus* was the so-called 'top predator', meaning that it was capable of attacking and eating any of the plant-eaters that lived at the time. Some earlier dinosaur communities did not have a top predator. *Megalosaurus* was big enough and had powerful enough jaws and hands to attack anything!

Buckland's drawing of the right lower jaw bone of *Megalosaurus*

NAMING A DINOSAUR

In 1824, *Megalosaurus* became the first dinosaur to be named anywhere in the world. William Buckland (1784–1856) did not collect the fossils himself. They were found by collectors near Oxford, England. However, he named the new animal *Megalosaurus*, meaning 'big lizard', which is more or less what he thought it was.

Anatomy of defence

The stegosaurs flourished in the Middle and Late Jurassic. They had a remarkable set of plates and spines, but experts disagree about whether these were for defence or for show.

Stegosaur armour was not perfect, because a theropod could nip in and bite their fleshy flanks. Maybe the spines made the animal look bigger than it actually was, causing a predator to think twice.

Like other stegosaurs, *Dacentrurus* had four fingers on each hand and three toes on each foot.

Dacentrurus

One of the first stegosaurs, *Dacentrurus* is best known from the Late Jurassic of Portugal, France and England. However, there are no complete skeletons. It was 6–10m long, and had two rows of small plates and spines down the middle of its back.

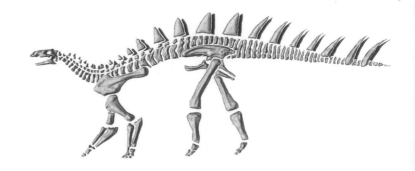

It is possible that, if attacked by a predatory dinosaur, *Dacentrurus* could have lashed out with its spiked tail.

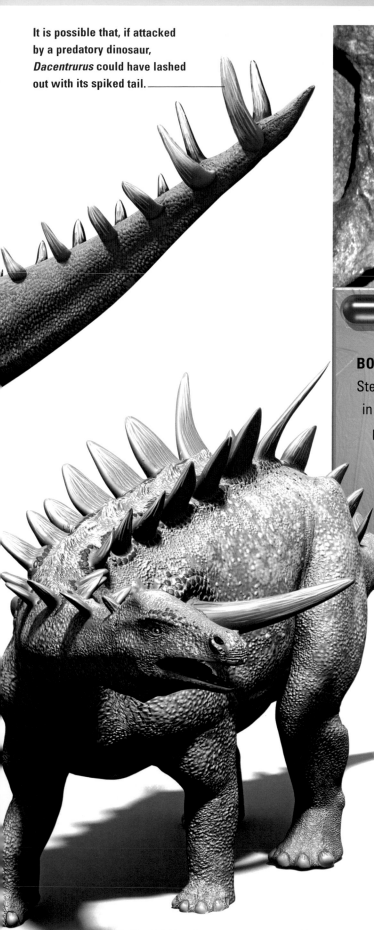

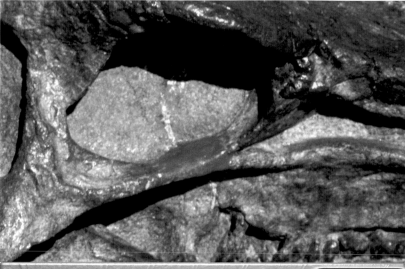

SCIENTIFIC
INPUT

BONES FOR PROTECTION
Stegosaurs had really tough skulls that were almost tubular in shape, and they protected famously tiny brains! This photograph shows a close-up of the eye socket, with a massive ridge over the top. There is also the back of the tooth ridge visible below, with its rows of small, triangular cheek teeth for grinding plant matter.

Huayangosaurus

This Chinese stegosaur was probably like *Dacentrurus*, but with differently shaped plates and spines. It was smaller, at only 4.5m long, and was probably preyed on by *Gasosaurus*. It is from the Zigong dinosaur sites (see pp.94–5), where 12 skeletons were found.

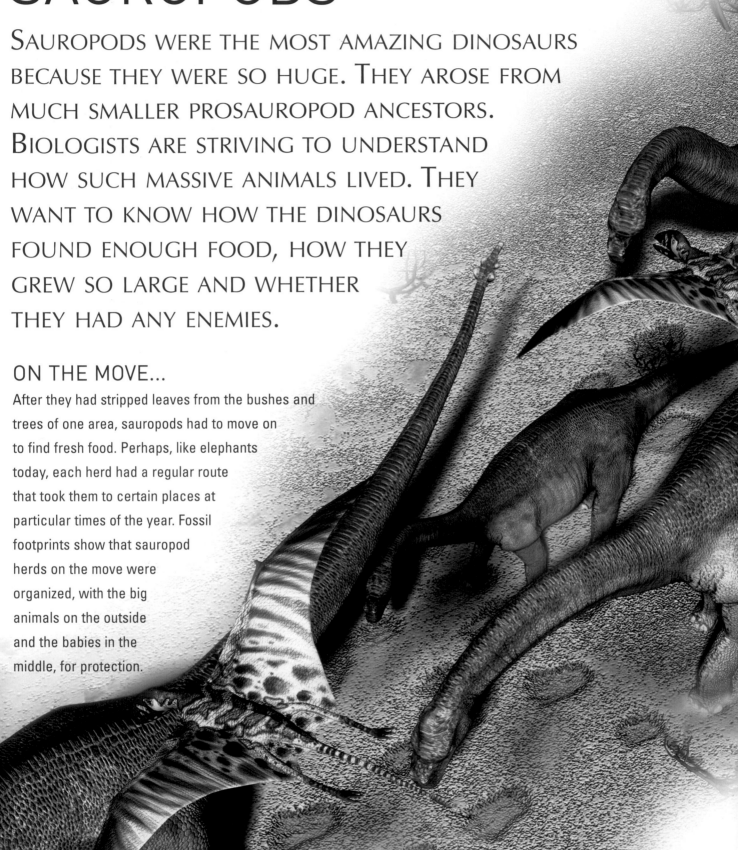

SAUROPODS

SAUROPODS WERE THE MOST AMAZING DINOSAURS BECAUSE THEY WERE SO HUGE. THEY AROSE FROM MUCH SMALLER PROSAUROPOD ANCESTORS. BIOLOGISTS ARE STRIVING TO UNDERSTAND HOW SUCH MASSIVE ANIMALS LIVED. THEY WANT TO KNOW HOW THE DINOSAURS FOUND ENOUGH FOOD, HOW THEY GREW SO LARGE AND WHETHER THEY HAD ANY ENEMIES.

ON THE MOVE...

After they had stripped leaves from the bushes and trees of one area, sauropods had to move on to find fresh food. Perhaps, like elephants today, each herd had a regular route that took them to certain places at particular times of the year. Fossil footprints show that sauropod herds on the move were organized, with the big animals on the outside and the babies in the middle, for protection.

Shunosaurus
11 tonnes

GIANTS ON EARTH

The early sauropods, such as
Shunosaurus and *Cetiosaurus* from the
Middle Jurassic, were medium-sized
sauropods. Later sauropods such as
Brachiosaurus may have weighed up to
50 tonnes. Baby sauropods were only a
metre or so long when they hatched, and they
probably grew to adult size in ten or twenty years.

Cetiosaurus
24 tonnes

DIET OF PLANTS

A 20-tonne sauropod had to eat a lot
of plants to survive. Tests on modern
relatives of Jurassic plants show that
horsetails, and some ferns and conifers,
were as nutritious as modern grasses,
so these were probably key elements in
the sauropod diet. However, cycads and
tree ferns have low nutritional value, and
so sauropods probably avoided them.

Cycad

Tree fern

Horsetails

In the laboratory

When it comes to finding clues about life in the past, tiny fossils can be as useful as giant bones.

Fossil hunters have to wash and sieve tonnes of sediment in the laboratory in order to separate out the teeth and bones of tiny creatures.

Hornsleasow

The Middle Jurassic of central England, UK, has produced amazing evidence of the smaller animals of the day. One site at Hornsleasow has proved especially rich. Ten tonnes of sand have preserved thousands of bones of fishes, frogs, salamanders, crocodilians and turtles that lived in small ponds, as well as plant remains.

The pointed tooth of the plant-eating *Stereognathus*, a small reptile closely related to the mammals

Hornsleasow fossils

The Hornsleasow fossils include crocodilians and small theropod dinosaurs that hunted early lizards and small mammals. The mammal fossils are very rare, but a few species have been identified that lived by feeding on insects. There are also a few bones of flying pterosaurs.

An artist's impression of the world of the animals of Hornsleasow

Sieving

Small fossils can be found by careful searching in the field, but sieving is better. Bags of sediment are washed to remove mud, and then carefully sieved. Small pieces of rubbish pass through the sieve, and the bones and teeth are left behind.

Drawings

Palaeontologists draw and photograph the fossils they find. Small fossils may be broken up, and the pieces can be put back together, so a drawing is made of the whole specimen, such as a skull (right).

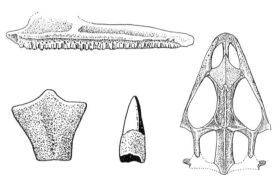

Microtomograph

Palaeontologists can now 'look inside' their fossils using a microtomograph. This machine makes virtual scans through the fossil, like slicing it up, and the scans can be put together by the computer to give a 3D image of the inside. This is very useful because it avoids damaging the fossil.

SEM scanning

The Scanning Electron Microscope (SEM) allows scientists to see great detail in tiny fossils, but also to make high-quality photographs, and even to analyse the chemical structures. It is very hard to make good photographs of tiny specimens under a normal light microscope because you can only focus on one level. In the SEM, you can see the full depth. If the preservation is unusual, some SEMs can do a chemical analysis.

SCIENTIFIC INPUT

PREPARING FOSSILS

Larger fossils are cut out of the rock in the field and wrapped in plaster and bandages to protect them. In the laboratory, the plaster parcels are cut open and the rock is carefully removed from the bones. This may require days of work with a small drill. Then each bone is coated with glues to harden it, and the whole skeleton can be assembled for display in a museum.

Dinosaur facts

Dinosaurs are well known because they broke all the records – they include the biggest land animals of all time! It can be difficult to establish accurate dinosaur measurements. Lengths are not hard, but it is very difficult to estimate weights.

LONGEST

• This is said to be *Amphicoelias*, estimated to be 40–60m long, but this dinosaur is known only from some isolated bones.
• The longest complete dinosaur that has been found is the sauropod *Supersaurus*, Late Jurassic, North America, which was 33–34m long (see pp.70–1).
• The longest predatory dinosaur was probably *Spinosaurus*, Early Cretaceous, North Africa, at some 14–18m in length, and weighing about 20 tonnes. This is much larger than *Tyrannosaurus rex*, which was 12–13m long and weighed 6–9 tonnes.

TALLEST

The tallest dinosaur was probably the sauropod *Brachiosaurus*, Late Jurassic, Tanzania (see pp.68–9), which was 25m long, but could raise its head to a height of about 13m above the ground.

HEAVIEST

• This may have been *Amphicoelias* at an estimated 120 tonnes, but this dinosaur is so incomplete that it is really impossible to be sure. More likely is the sauropod *Argentinosaurus* from the middle Cretaceous of Argentina, some 30m long, and weighing an estimated 73–88 tonnes.

SMALLEST

• This was the tiny duck-sized theropod *Mei long*, Early Cretaceous, China, measuring only 53cm in length and weighing less than 70g.

DINOSAUR EGGS

• The largest dinosaur eggs are 30cm long and 25.5cm all round, and they can hold about 3.3 litres of water. These are eggs laid by sauropod dinosaurs, and they were found in southern France and Argentina.
• The smallest dinosaur eggs were reported in 2005 from the Cretaceous of Thailand. They are 18mm long, and smaller than the eggs of a sparrow.

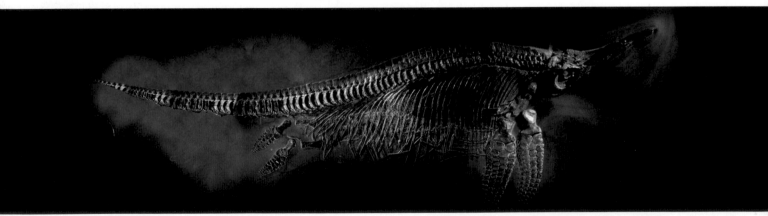

The fossil of an *Ichthyosaurus* mother with five unborn babies

WEBSITES ON RECORD-BREAKING DINOSAURS

http://en.wikipedia.org/wiki/Dinosaur_size All the records.

www.nhm.ac.uk/nature-online/life/dinosaurs-other-extinct-creatures/dino-directory/ In-depth information.

www.enchantedlearning.com/subjects/dinosaurs/questions/faq/Smallest.shtml Questions answered.

www.livescience.com/animals/060301_big_carnivores.html Dinosaurs in the news.

THE TIME OF THE GIANTS

The Late Jurassic was the time of giant dinosaurs. Great sauropods such as *Diplodocus* and *Brachiosaurus* stomped around the world, feeding on cycads and tree ferns. Armoured dinosaurs and small and large theropods made up the ecosystems. Amazing new flying and swimming reptiles also came on the scene during this period.

Jurassic giant

The largest known dinosaur is *Brachiosaurus*, found first in North America in 1903. This monster dinosaur's name means 'arm lizard', because of its incredible neck.

The first fossils from Wyoming, USA, were several vertebrae and limb bones, and these suggested a real monster. Then Werner Janensch visited Tanzania and found much more complete material (see pp.68–9).

Fossil skull

The skull of *Brachiosaurus* is full of holes! Like many other sauropods, the nostrils are not at the tip of the snout, but up between the eye sockets. The high-placed nostrils suggested that these sauropods lived underwater, and breathed through the top of the head.

Experts believe that the skull of *Brachiosaurus* had many holes in order to reduce its weight, and the overall weight of this massive beast's head.

The neck and head were probably held out in front of the dinosaur, but could stretch up as high as 13m to reach leaves in tall trees.

Land or water?

The greatest mystery about giant dinosaurs such as *Brachiosaurus* is how they survived. The world they lived in was more or less the same as today's, and they had to carry their vast weight of 50 tonnes. This is why many palaeontologists thought they lived in the water, so they could float. However, fossil footprints prove that they lived on land.

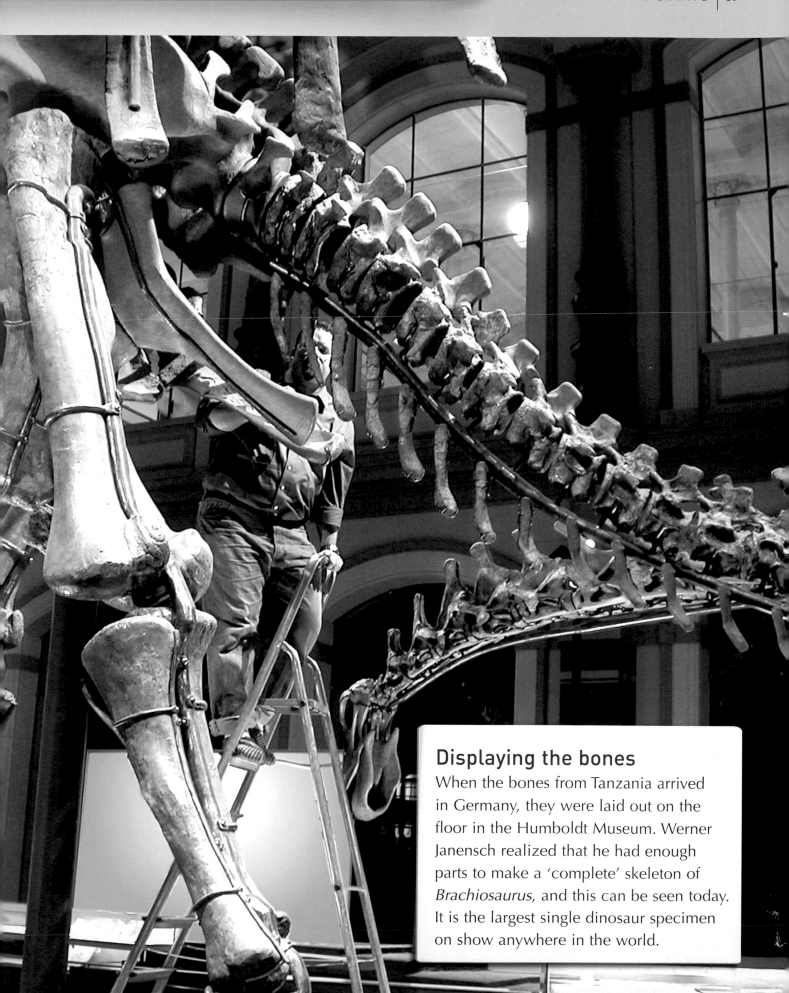

Displaying the bones

When the bones from Tanzania arrived in Germany, they were laid out on the floor in the Humboldt Museum. Werner Janensch realized that he had enough parts to make a 'complete' skeleton of *Brachiosaurus*, and this can be seen today. It is the largest single dinosaur specimen on show anywhere in the world.

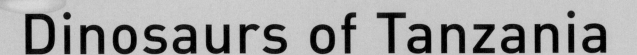

Dinosaurs of Tanzania

The Tendaguru deposits in Tanzania have produced an amazing series of dinosaur skeletons. At the time they were discovered, nobody expected to find dinosaurs in Africa.

In about 1900, this area was a German colony. Geologists had reported huge bones around a hill called Tendaguru, and in 1909–13, the Humboldt Museum in Berlin, Germany, ran expeditions.

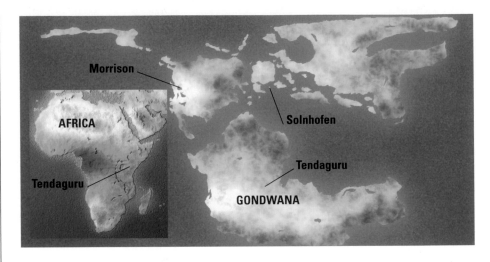

Tendaguru on the map

Tendaguru lies 100km inland in eastern Africa (small map). In the Jurassic (main map), the hill lay in the middle of the continent Gondwana. The dinosaurs are very like those of the Morrison Formation in North America (see pp.74–5), and dinosaurs could walk across narrow land bridges linking the continents. Solnhofen in Europe has some of the same pterosaurs (see pp.82–3).

Werner Janensch

The Tendaguru expeditions were led by Werner Janensch (1878–1969), curator at the Humboldt Museum. He spent 50 years studying the new dinosaurs that had been found.

Dryosaurus

The ornithopod *Dryosaurus* was discovered in the Morrison Formation in 1878. It fed on low plants, and probably relied on speed to escape from predators. Remains of the same dinosaur were found at Tendaguru – clear evidence of the land link.

Dryosaurus ranged in size from 2.5m to 4.5m in length.

Raising its head would have been difficult for any length of time.

Barosaurus measured up to 27m from head to tip of tail.

Elaphrosaurus

One of the more unusual predators from Tendaguru is *Elaphrosaurus*, named by Janensch in 1920. This slender, 6m-long animal had powerful jaws and slim fingers for grabbing its prey. It may have hunted smaller dinosaurs such as *Dryosaurus*, as well as lizards and mammals.

New finds at Tendaguru

Some new expeditions to Tendaguru in the last few years have turned up fossils of smaller animals such as pterosaurs and mammals. But the earlier trips 100 years ago had been so thorough that they had cleared out all of the dinosaur bones!

Barosaurus

This dinosaur was reported first in North America in 1890, and then in Tendaguru in 1908. This sauropod may have swung its head high to reach leaves in the tops of trees, but this neck position may have created problems for blood flow. So *Barosaurus* probably kept its head down, at the level of its shoulders, for most of the time.

THE BIGGEST DINOSAURS

THE SAUROPODS WERE THE BIGGEST DINOSAURS. SOME MAY HAVE WEIGHED OVER 60 TONNES. THE BIGGEST ELEPHANT TODAY WEIGHS 6 TONNES, SO THEY WERE UP TO TEN TIMES BIGGER!

JENSEN AND *SUPERSAURUS*

The huge size of some sauropods is shown by this fossil shoulder blade. Its discoverer, Jim Jensen, lying beside the bone, was some 2m tall. He found the bones in the Morrison Formation of Colorado, USA, in 1972, and called this enormous dinosaur *Supersaurus*. One theory is that *Supersaurus* might just be a large example of *Diplodocus*. But most experts now accept that it was definitely a sauropod dinosaur, and that the fossil includes remains of another dinosaur named *Ultrasauros* by Jensen.

This parade of sauropods includes all of the giants: *Amphicoelias* (up to 60m), *Argentinosaurus* (up to 30m), *Bruhathkayosaurus* (up to 34m), *Diplodocus* (up to 35m), *Sauroposeidon* (up to 17m), and *Supersaurus* (up to 34m).

■ *Amphicoelias*	■ *Bruhathkayosaurus*
■ *Diplodocus*	■ *Argentinosaurus*
■ *Supersaurus*	■ *Sauroposeidon*

PARADE OF THE GIANTS

Sauropods varied from 7m to 60m in length, and there has been a long debate about which was actually the largest. Many sauropod skeletons are incomplete, and some of the largest are known from only a few leg bones or vertebrae from the backbone. The largest complete skeletons are *Brachiosaurus* and *Diplodocus*. *Supersaurus*, *Argentinosaurus* or *Amphicoelias* may have been even larger.

Bone wars

The great 'bone wars' lasted 20 years. Two palaeontologists, rushing to be the first to name new animals, scrapped over all the new dinosaur fossils found in the western USA.

Cope and Marsh began as friends, working together until 1870. Then they squabbled over the rights to a particular dig site, and their teams came to blows.

Othniel Charles Marsh
Marsh (right, on the left) was a professor at Yale University. He named 80 new species of dinosaurs, including *Allosaurus* and *Diplodocus*, as well as the Cretaceous bird *Ichthyornis*.

Edward Drinker Cope
Cope was a professor at the Academy of Natural Sciences in Philadelphia. He published 1,200 scientific papers, and named more than 70 dinosaur species, including *Camarasaurus* and *Coelophysis*.

Early field teams
Marsh and Cope paid railroad men, and others, to dig up bones. These men put them in wooden crates and sent them back east by railroad. There was no time to map the site or protect the bones.

Apatosaurus

Marsh named *Apatosaurus* in 1877, based on some isolated bones of a huge animal from the Morrison Formation (see pp.74–5). Because the remains were so incomplete, he could not say much about what the animal was or how it lived, but he knew it was a sauropod.

Marsh knew *Apatosaurus* was different from the other finds in the Morrison Formation.

Brontosaurus

Two years later, in 1879, Marsh named *Brontosaurus*, and this name, meaning 'thunder lizard', became popular. However, in 1903, another palaeontologist realized that the two animals were one and the same, so the older name, *Apatosaurus*, has priority, and is the one used today.

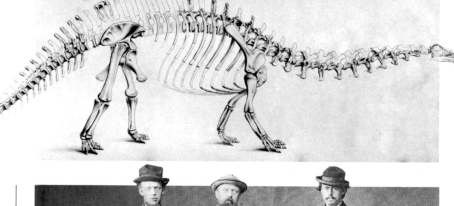

Changing heads

For years, *Apatosaurus* was given the head of *Camarasaurus*. In 1975, a careful study of a skeleton showed that *Apatosaurus* was a relative of *Diplodocus*, with its long snout (above). All the heads in museum displays had to be changed!

HISTORICAL DATA

ARMED TO THE TEETH

The 1870s and 1880s were still the days of the 'Wild West', and the fossil diggers had to go armed with rifles. This picture shows Marsh – he is the bearded man in the centre of the back row – with his team. These hardy men slept in tents, even in the freezing winters. Marsh paid them by results, and they had to fight off bad weather, grizzly bears and rival bone-diggers.

THE MORRISON FORMATION

The Morrison Formation of the Midwestern USA has been one of the richest sources of dinosaur fossils since the 'Bone Wars' began in the 1870s (see pp.72–3).

MORRISON MAMMALS

The Morrison Formation has not only yielded specimens of dinosaurs, but also plants, fishes and other land animals. The Morrison mammals include several small, shrew-like animals with sharp, needle-like teeth. They probably hunted insects such as beetles.

MORRISON ROCKS

The rocks of the Morrison Formation are sandstones and mudstones, mainly deposited by ancient rivers. Dinosaur skeletons are mostly found in ancient sand bars, deposits of sand in the middle of rivers. When heavy rains fell, the rivers became raging torrents, and dead animals and plants were swept away. As the flow slowed, the remains were dumped on sand banks at the edges and in the middle of the rivers.

MORRISON LANDSCAPE

Allosaurus, *Diplodocus*, *Stegosaurus* and *Ornitholestes* move about on the river plain surrounded by a lush vegetation of horsetails and ferns in the marshy areas, and ginkgo and conifer trees on more stable ground. The top predator, *Allosaurus* (right), is eyeing up the unsuspecting *Stegosaurus* (left) – perhaps for his next meal. The small pack of *Ornitholestes* in the distance may be on the lookout for prey as well.

Stegosaurus

Stegosaurus is one of the best-known dinosaurs found in the Morrison Formation. It was one of the first armoured, plant-eating dinosaurs to be studied in detail.

The plates down its back have caused endless debates. They did not protect its sides, but they made it look bigger. They were probably covered in skin and may have been brightly coloured.

Stegosaurus **had a tiny, tubular skull and jaws lined with small, leaf-shaped teeth for snipping plants.**

Armoured plates

The bony plates began behind the head, and ran down the back to spikes at the end of the tail. Each plate stood in the skin and muscle of the back – not connected to the backbone. They were probably upright, and could not be moved about.

Reconstruction

At one time, palaeontologists wondered whether there was a single row of plates, or whether they stood out sideways, forming a kind of bony sunshade. New specimens show their upright pattern, and the short arms show that the head was carried close to the ground, while the tail was raised quite high.

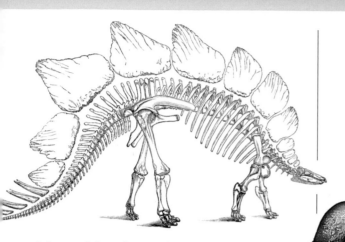

Ankylosaurus

Stegosaurus

Diplodocus

Marsh's drawing

When Othniel Marsh named *Stegosaurus* in 1877, he had a fairly complete skeleton, and his artist was able to make a reconstruction drawing (above). The idea of how *Stegosaurus* looked has not changed much since then, despite the unearthing of new specimens.

Tail spikes

Different dinosaurs had different weapons on their tails. Ankylosaurs sometimes had great bony clubs for hitting their enemies. *Stegosaurus* had sharp spikes on its tail, probably also for defence. Most dinosaurs, though, had no clubs or spikes (above right), and probably just used their tails for balance, and for sweeping away clouds of flies.

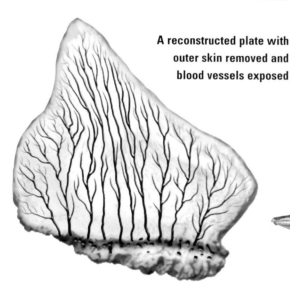

A reconstructed plate with outer skin removed and blood vessels exposed

Kentrosaurus was up to 4m long, and its name means 'pointed lizard'.

Blood flow

We know that *Stegosaurus'* plates were covered with skin because there are canals for blood vessels on each side. The blood flowed through the skin, and *Stegosaurus* could probably have flushed the plates red.

Kentrosaurus

There were many other stegosaurs that have been found in different places. Another well-known stegosaur is *Kentrosaurus*, from Tanzania. It looks like *Stegosaurus*, but it was not as big, with only small plates at the front, and many spikes on the back and down the tail.

Allosaurus

The giant theropods were killing machines with fearsome claws and jaws that had a powerful bite.

The fossils tell us that theropods such as *Allosaurus* ate meat, and kill sites show which dinosaurs they ate. But how is the power of their jaws and bite force measured?

Fossil tooth

Allosaurus had massive, curved teeth with a pointed tip and a sharp edge front and back, divided into zig-zags like the edge of a steak knife. This tooth could cut through bone!

MEASURING FORCES

Finite element analysis is a technique used by engineers to test the strength of bridges and buildings, but it can be used on animals, too.

The skull is scanned into a computer using a laser scanner.

The skull scan is converted into a 3D mesh of imaginary cells.

Forces are applied to the mesh's cells to test how the skull behaves.

Stresses and strains

Finite element analysis allows palaeontologists to model the forces on dinosaur skulls. The computer model shows the effects of biting on *Allosaurus*' skull. The 'colder' the colours are (blue and green), the more bite force there was.

Allosaurus could bite hard, but not as hard as expected.

Allosaurus attack

Although *Allosaurus* had a weaker bite than expected, its skull was built to withstand huge forces. It probably used its head like an axe, opening the jaws and hacking down hard. It could break bones and cause even a large sauropod to bleed to death.

Supreme hunter

Allosaurus had three sets of weapons that it used to catch and kill its prey: jaws, feet and hands. The jaws were used first, to bite and hack at the prey – even a quick swipe would disable it. *Allosaurus* then moved in and stopped the prey struggling with its massive feet. Finally, it used hands and jaws to tear off meat.

Fearsome claws

Allosaurus had long, powerful fingers and sharp claws. Its arms were quite short, so the hands were probably not used for attack or killing.

DINOSAURS AND DRIFT

DINOSAURS ORIGINATED ON A SINGLE SUPERCONTINENT CALLED PANGAEA, IN THE TRIASSIC, AND THE ATLANTIC OCEAN BEGAN TO OPEN UP DURING THE JURASSIC AND CRETACEOUS. THE SCIENTIFIC EVIDENCE FOR CONTINENTAL DRIFT IS OVERWHELMING.

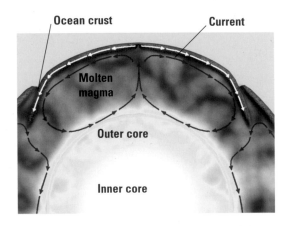

Ocean crust
Current
Molten magma
Outer core
Inner core

WHY PLATES PART

Continental drift is driven by plate tectonics. Beneath the solid crust, the Earth is molten. Great currents move within this molten magma in slow circles, pulling the central ocean crust apart at a rate of about 1cm per year.

SHARED DINOSAURS

One of the key pieces of evidence for continental drift is the distribution of dinosaurs. For example, the ornithopod *Dryosaurus* and the sauropod *Barosaurus* occurred in both Africa and North America, because the two continents were joined together in the Jurassic.

Dryosaurus

NORTH AMERICA

North Atlantic Ocean

AFRICA

Pacific Ocean

SOUTH AMERICA

South Atlantic Ocean

ANTARCTICA

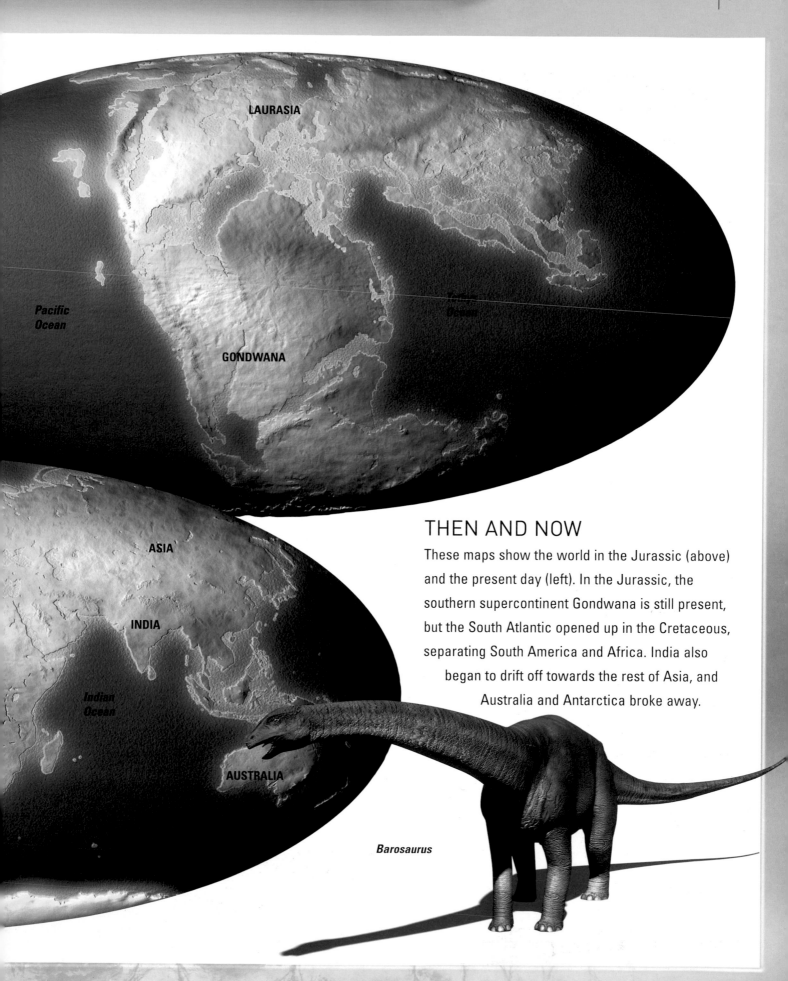

LAURASIA

Pacific
Ocean

GONDWANA

ASIA

INDIA

Indian
Ocean

AUSTRALIA

Barosaurus

THEN AND NOW

These maps show the world in the Jurassic (above) and the present day (left). In the Jurassic, the southern supercontinent Gondwana is still present, but the South Atlantic opened up in the Cretaceous, separating South America and Africa. India also began to drift off towards the rest of Asia, and Australia and Antarctica broke away.

The Solnhofen lagoon

The details of ancient life often come from unique sites where delicate fossils have been preserved. The Solnhofen lagoon of southern Germany shows us another side to Jurassic life.

Stonemasons found the first fossils in Solnhofen hundreds of years ago. The site was made famous by the discovery of the early bird *Archaeopteryx*.

The lagoon

The rocks at Solnhofen are thin limestones. There are fossils of animals that lived in the shallow, warm seas, as well as some land plants, rare dinosaurs, insects, birds and pterosaurs.

The Solnhofen quarries

German stonemasons have been extracting thin limestone slabs from the Solnhofen quarries for centuries. The slabs are so fine-grained that, in the past, they have been used for printing (see left). Today, they are used for building.

Fossil finds

Many thousands of spectacular fossils have been found in the Solnhofen quarries over the past 200 years. As the workmen split the thin slabs of limestone, they often find delicate fossils. When split, some slabs have a beautiful impression of the fossil on both halves, like this fish.

Teeming with life

The Solnhofen lagoon was full of fishes, shrimps (below), jellyfish, shellfish, corals and other sea creatures. Dozens of kinds of insects were preyed on by *Archaeopteryx*. Most of the pterosaurs fed on fishes, which they snapped out of the water.

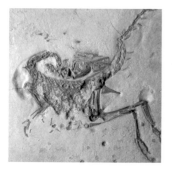

This original specimen of *Compsognathus* is complete, and shows the head bending back over the body.

Compsognathus

The only dinosaur from Solnhofen is *Compsognathus*, a small flesh-eater, known from a single specimen that was found in 1850. This delicate, 1m-long animal fed on small prey, such as lizards or mammals on land. It probably fished for tasty shrimps and fishes in the shallow, warm waters of the lagoon.

Archaeopteryx

The most famous fossil in the world is probably that of *Archaeopteryx*, considered to be the 'missing link' between dinosaurs and birds.

HAND EVOLUTION

There are enough fossils to show, step by step, how a theropod dinosaur evolved into a bird.

The oldest theropods had four or five fingers on each of their hands.

Later theropods had only three or two fingers on each hand.

Dromaeosaurids had long fingers with large claws.

Archaeopteryx had slender fingers, like the dromaeosaurids.

In modern birds, the fingers are thin and there are no claws.

The first fossils of this 'early bird' were found in 1860 in Solnhofen, Germany. Since then, ten fossil skeletons from the Late Jurassic have been discovered, also in Germany.

The first bird

Palaeontologists have debated for years how well *Archaeopteryx* could fly. Studies of models in wind tunnels show that it could fly very well, but it was probably not as good at dodging through the trees as a modern bird.

Only baby hoatzins have claws.

The hoatzin

This unusual bird from South America lays its eggs in rough nests in trees that overhang the rivers. If a predatory hawk approaches, the hoatzin babies clamber away from the nest, using claws on their hands. This feature gives us a strong hint that all birds once had claws on their hands.

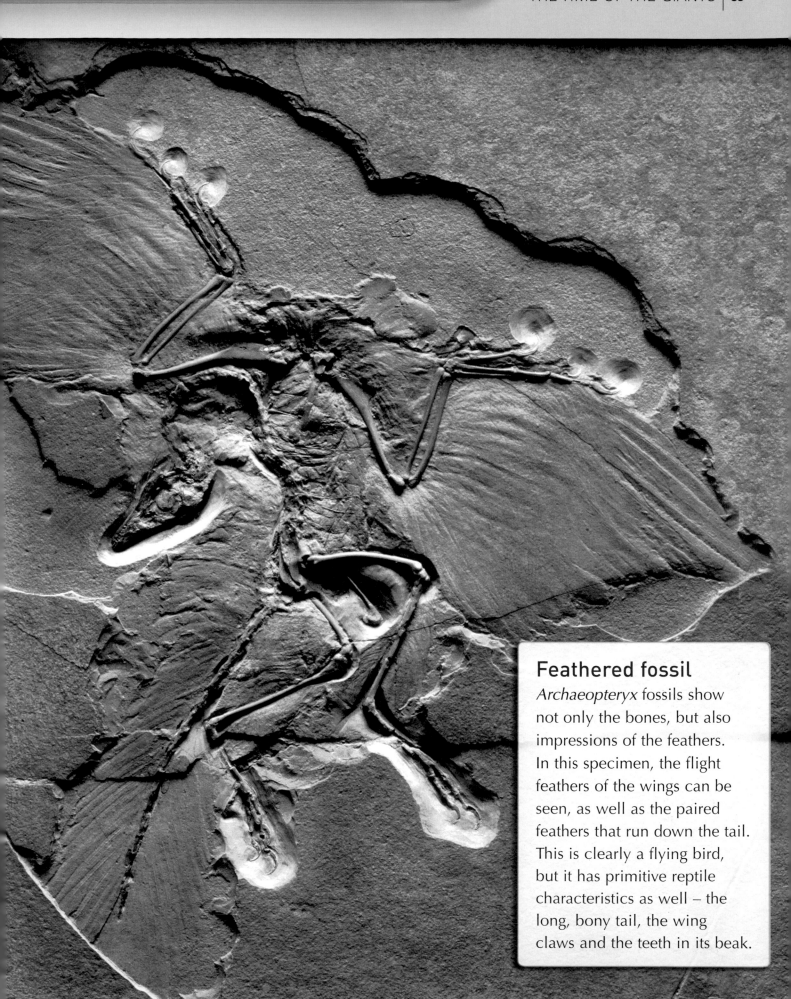

Feathered fossil

Archaeopteryx fossils show not only the bones, but also impressions of the feathers. In this specimen, the flight feathers of the wings can be seen, as well as the paired feathers that run down the tail. This is clearly a flying bird, but it has primitive reptile characteristics as well – the long, bony tail, the wing claws and the teeth in its beak.

FLYING REPTILES

PTEROSAURS WERE EXTRAORDINARY REPTILES.
THEY WERE NOT DINOSAURS, BUT THEY WERE
CLOSE RELATIVES. THEY LIVED THROUGH THE
SAME TIME SPAN, FROM THE LATE TRIASSIC TO
THE LATE CRETACEOUS. PTEROSAURS HAD LONG
WINGS FORMED BY AN EXTENDED FOURTH
FINGER ON THE HAND, WHICH SUPPORTED
A THIN, TOUGH WING MADE FROM SKIN.

FOSSIL FINDS

Some of the best specimens
of pterosaurs are known from
the Solnhofen lagoon of the
Late Jurassic. They were found in the same
rocks as *Archaeopteryx* (see pp.84–5). Some
specimens, such as this one, show all the
bones of the delicate skeleton, as well as clear
impressions of the wing membranes. Some
even show that the wings were made from
several layers of skin, with toughening fibres,
and that the body was covered with hair.

**Two *Ctenochasma* spread
their wings to dry.**

A flock of *Pterodactylus* head out to sea to find fish to eat.

The wingspan of *Rhamphorynchus* was up to 1.8m.

PTEROSAURS OF THE LAGOON

The first Solnhofen pterosaur specimen was reported in 1784. Since then, hundreds of specimens have been found, and dozens named. In fact, there were probably six or seven species of pterosaur flapping slowly over the Solnhofen lagoon, ranging in size from a blackbird to a large seagull. Most fed on fish that they snapped up from the shallow, clear water. On the ground, pterosaurs moved awkwardly, and fossil footprints show that they walked on all fours, using their wing-hands to keep themselves from toppling over.

Dinosaurs of Portugal

Since 1990, there have been some really good fossil finds in Portugal. They show that the country shared dinosaurs not only with the rest of Europe, but also with North America.

Some of the dinosaurs are known only in Portugal, but others are familiar in France and England. The discovery of species also found in North America came as a surprise.

Lourinhanosaurus

A partial skeleton of this flesh-eater was found in 1998. It could be related to *Allosaurus* from North America, or to *Megalosaurus* from England – no one is sure. It is important not to confuse *Lourinhanosaurus* with *Lourinhasaurus*, a sauropod that is also from Portugal.

Dinheirosaurus

Many sauropods have been found in Portugal, but most of the finds are only of parts of the skeleton. *Dinheirosaurus* was named in 1999, based on a series of vertebrae from its spine (below). The vertebrae are like those from the backbone of *Diplodocus*.

The spikes along the tail were fixed deep into the skin and muscle, and would have deterred predators.

Dacentrurus

By the Late Jurassic, stegosaurs were known worldwide (see pp.76–7). *Dacentrurus* is a stegosaur that has been unearthed in several parts of Europe, and it was found in Portugal in the 1990s. The armour consists of small plates at the front, and long spikes further back.

Torvosaurus probably held its prey down with its massive, three-toed feet as it tore at the flesh with its jaws.

Torvosaurus

When *Torvosaurus* was found in Portugal, it was already well known from the Morrison Formation of North America. Here was key evidence that the north Atlantic had still not opened very wide, and that dinosaurs could migrate across. This giant predator weighed 2 tonnes, and could have hunted the sauropods.

Octavio Mateus

Mateus has run dinosaur excavations in Portugal since 1991, mainly near the town of Lourinha.

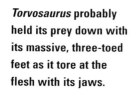

His work has revealed a whole new dinosaur fauna that was barely known before, and he has named seven new dinosaurs.

Footprints by the shore

There are many long dinosaur trackways in late Jurassic rocks along Portugal's Atlantic coastline. Here, Octavio Mateus is pointing to a series of footprints, one of the 17 trackways found at this site.

EARTH EVIDENCE

A YOUNG PALAEONTOLOGIST

Palaeontologists of all ages can make great discoveries. Eleven-year-old Jacob Walen of the Netherlands is holding a piece of a dinosaur's jaw bone next to a reconstructed skull of *Torvosaurus* at the Lourinha Museum. He found the jawbone in 2003, when he was only six, while on holiday in Portugal with his family, and gave the fossil to the museum in 2008. His discovery is now famous – it was reported all around the world.

Marine reptiles

The Late Jurassic was a time when great reptiles swam in the seas. Ichthyosaurs and crocodiles hunted fishes and squid, and in turn were eaten by large pliosaurs.

Fossils of these sea monsters have been found in many parts of the world. Some have the remains of their last meal in their stomachs.

Liopleurodon

Biggest of all was *Liopleurodon*. Complete skulls indicate that it was up to 10m long, but some isolated bones suggest that individuals may have reached 15m. These huge reptiles, as big as modern whales, were the top predators of their day.

Metriorhynchus

Crocodiles today are water-lovers. Jurassic crocodiles such as *Metriorhynchus* could swim really well, their arms and legs acting as paddles. *Metriorhynchus* had a fin at the end of its tail, just like a fish, and would have had great difficulty walking on land.

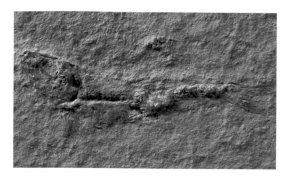

Fossil fish

Many of the marine reptiles fed on fish. Some Jurassic fish fossils, such as this one from Solnhofen (see pp.82–3), show great detail. The Jurassic was a time of change, as older, heavier fishes gave way to the new teleosts – lighter and faster fishes such as the modern herring and salmon.

Pliosaurus

A close relative of *Liopleurodon*, *Pliosaurus* was smaller, ranging in length from 2m to 10m. These sea monsters breathed air, so perhaps they threw their prey in the air to stun them, as killer whales do today.

Belemnites had long, fleshy tails and fins at the side to keep their balance in the water as they swam.

Belemnites

These creatures are related to modern cuttlefish and squid, as well as to the fossil ammonites (see p.47). Belemnites had a shell, but it was internal and shaped like a bullet. The fleshy body had tentacles for catching food.

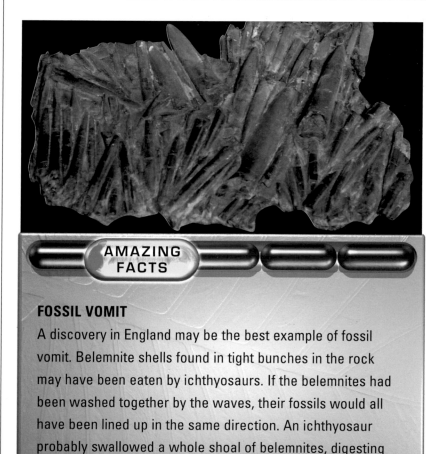

AMAZING FACTS

FOSSIL VOMIT

A discovery in England may be the best example of fossil vomit. Belemnite shells found in tight bunches in the rock may have been eaten by ichthyosaurs. If the belemnites had been washed together by the waves, their fossils would all have been lined up in the same direction. An ichthyosaur probably swallowed a whole shoal of belemnites, digesting their soft tissues and then spitting up the hard shells.

Chinese dinosaurs

Recent finds in China have amazed the world – there are so many new dinosaurs and other fossils.

Palaeontologists reported the first dinosaurs from China only in the 1920s, 100 years after the first finds in Europe. Today, new Chinese finds are reported all the time.

Dong Zhiming

One of the most active Chinese paleontologists has been Dong Zhiming. From 1973 to 2009, he named 26 new dinosaurs, including most of the Late Jurassic dinosaurs on these pages. He found several key dinosaur sites, including Dashanpu.

Huayangosaurus **was 4.5m long.**

Huayangosaurus

One of Dong Zhiming's Dashanpu discoveries is the remarkable stegosaur *Huayangosaurus*. Twelve skeletons have been found. Unlike its relative *Stegosaurus* (see pp.76–7), *Huayangosaurus* has spikes all along its back.

Shunosaurus

Another of Dong Zhiming's discoveries at Dashanpu, *Shunosaurus* was a 10m-long sauropod. So far, 20 skeletons have been found, so this is actually one of the best-known sauropod dinosaurs in the world. Its name means 'Shu lizard'.

Xiaosaurus

This small, plant-eating dinosaur may be related to *Lesothosaurus* from South Africa (see p.34). It is known only from teeth and a few isolated bones.

Xuanhanosaurus

This theropod was 6m long, and probably preyed on *Xiaosaurus* and other smaller dinosaurs. *Xuanhanosaurus* had remarkably long arms, probably for grabbing and grappling with prey, rather than for walking on all fours. The incomplete fossils suggest that it may be a relative of *Megalosaurus* (see pp.56–7) and *Allosaurus* (see pp.78–9).

Yangchuanosaurus's teeth descended past its jaw line when its mouth was shut.

Yangchuanosaurus

The largest predator in the Dashanpu area, *Yangchuanosaurus* is known from a complete skeleton (above), found in 1977. This dinosaur was 8–10m long, and had short arms, with three fingers on each hand. It had a narrow skull, deep, powerful jaws and a low, bony crest along its snout – possibly for display. It was named by Dong Zhiming.

The Zigong dinosaurs

Some of the best Chinese fossils are from the Middle Jurassic Shaximiao Formation in Zigong Province.

The first fossils were found in 1972 when a Chinese gas company found the bones of a theropod, later called *Gasosaurus*.

Gasosaurus

This theropod was up to 4m long and is a little like *Megalosaurus* (see pp.56–7). Its skull has not been found, so a reconstruction was made for display in the Zigong Museum.

Omeisaurus

There were several sauropods in the Shaximiao Formation, including *Omeisaurus*, which was up to 15m long and weighed 4 tonnes. This dinosaur was first reported in 1939, and since then many species from the Middle and Late Jurassic have been found in different locations in China.

A gap in the record

For a long time, the Middle Jurassic was a mystery because its dinosaurs were not well known. The only finds were in Europe, and there were no discoveries in North America. The findings in Zigong Province in the 1970s filled the gap, and showed that China had similar dinosaurs to those found in England.

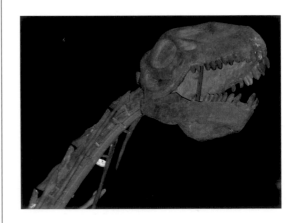

Datousaurus

This sauropod was also 15m long. It had a relatively large skull, with spoon-shaped teeth in the jaws. Its name means 'big head reptile'. *Datousaurus* and *Omeisaurus* may have fed on different plants, so they would not have been in competition.

The Zigong Dinosaur Museum

One of the most amazing dinosaur displays is in Zigong, where the palaeontologists decided to preserve part of the original bone bed as a permanent exhibit. They found so many bones in one place that a roof could be built over the dinosaur graveyard. Visitors can see the technicians cleaning up the bones where they lie.

Dinosaur facts

About 1,500 species of dinosaurs have been named since 1824, and a new dinosaur is named every two or three weeks. Many of the older identifications turn out to be incorrect, or are based on remains that cannot be identified.

THE FIRST DINOSAUR

• Some very scrappy remains, from the Middle Triassic (235 mya) were found in Madagascar, the island off the west coast of Africa, and reported in 1999. The remains may be those of a very ancient dinosaur.

• The oldest confirmed fossils are *Eoraptor* and *Herrerasaurus*, from the Late Triassic (230 mya) Ischigualasto Formation of Argentina (see pp.16–17).

THE LAST DINOSAURS

• Fossils of *Tyrannosaurus rex* and *Triceratops* are found in the last few metres of the Hell Creek Formation, Montana, USA, in the very last years of the Cretaceous, just below the great mass extinction level (see p.149).

SHORTEST DINOSAUR NAME

• *Mei*, from the species *Mei long*, which means 'sleeping dragon'. This was an early troodontid from the Early Cretaceous, China, and was named by Xing Xu and Mark Norell in 2004.

LONGEST DINOSAUR NAME

• *Micropachycephalosaurus*, from the species *Micropachycephalosaurus hongtuyanensis*, which means 'tiny thick-headed reptile from Hongtuyan'. This was a small pachycephalosaur from the Late Cretaceous of China, and was named by the Chinese palaeontologist Dong Zhiming in 1978.

FIRST DINOSAUR TO BE NAMED

• *Megalosaurus*, which was named by William Buckland in 1824. This was a large theropod from the Middle Jurassic of England.

LAST DINOSAUR TO BE NAMED

It is impossible to say because a new dinosaur species is named about every two weeks somewhere in the world. Look up 'Wikipedia: Dinosaurs', or any other search engine, and type in 'new dinosaur, this month', and see what comes up!

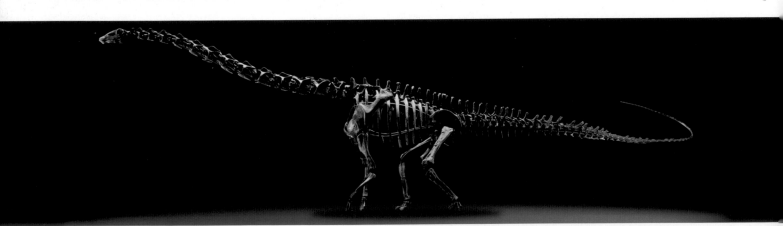

A *Diplodocus* from Wyoming, USA, originally described by palaeontologist OC Marsh

WEBSITES ON THE HISTORY OF PALAEONTOLOGISTS AND DINOSAUR NAMING

http://palaeo.gly.bris.ac.uk/Palaeofiles/History/index.html   All the historical dinosaur hunters.

http://academic.brooklyn.cuny.edu/geology/chamber/dinohist1.html   More on dinosaur hunters.

http://en.wikipedia.org/wiki/Portal:Dinosaurs   Access to information on many dinosaurs.

http://en.wikipedia.org/wiki/List_of_dinosaurs   Check this list for the latest dinosaurs.

A FLOWERING WORLD

The Early Cretaceous was a time of change. The giant sauropods of the Late Jurassic were replaced as the main plant-eaters by ornithopods such as *Iguanodon*. The world also began to modernize in a big way, with the spread of flowering plants, insects such as bees and butterflies, frogs, lizards, snakes, birds and mammals.

The Cretaceous world

In the Cretaceous, the giant dinosaurs of the Late Jurassic gave way to plant-eating ornithopod dinosaurs, and many exciting new plants and animals.

Modern ecosystems developed during the Cretaceous. Lizards, birds and mammals became more dominant, and flowering plants, ants, bees and snakes appeared.

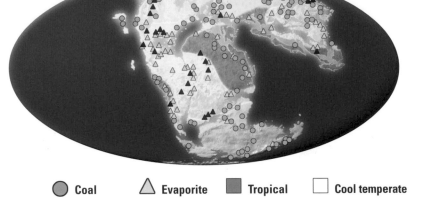

- ● Coal
- ▲ Calcrete
- △ Evaporite
- ■ Tropical
- □ Arid
- □ Cool temperate
- □ Warm temperate

The Wealden scene

Early examples of these new ecosystems may be seen in the Early Cretaceous of southeast England, in rocks called the Wealden Group. There were still some sauropods around, but the landscape was dominated by ornithopod dinosaurs, such as *Iguanodon* and *Hypsilophodon*, that browsed on low plants. There was also a new predator – *Baryonyx*, a long-snouted spinosaurid (below left).

A warmer world

The Cretaceous was warmer than today. Widespread coal shows it was a hot and wet climate, with arid desert beds and calcretes (limestone soils). There was probably no ice at the poles except in midwinter.

The Wealden in the UK

The Wealden rocks are to be seen south of London (right). Geologists have studied them for hundreds of years, and the first dinosaur bones were found in the 1820s. Since then, palaeontologists have found thousands of fossil plants, mammals, fishes, lizards, shellfish and dinosaurs.

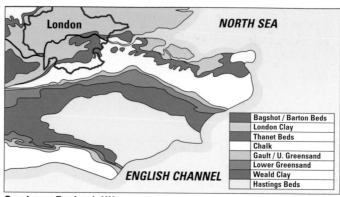

| | Bagshot / Barton Beds |
| London Clay |
| Thanet Beds |
| Chalk |
| Gault / U. Greensand |
| Lower Greensand |
| Weald Clay |
| Hastings Beds |

Southeast England, UK

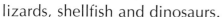

Wealden plants

Dozens of different plant fossils have been found in the Wealden rocks. Low-growing ferns and horsetails grew in damp areas beside rivers and ponds, together with bushy and tree-like plants such as cycads, ginkgos and conifers. This fossil frond (left) is named *Zamites*. It was a cycad that looked like a giant pineapple, and it had dozens of fronds sprouting from the top.

Fossil finds

The Wealden rocks were laid down in rivers and lakes of a great low-lying coastal landscape. Some of the fish, such as *Lepidotes* (below), were quite large. This fish was up to 50cm long and had regular rows of thick, squarish, bony scales. Even with such an armour, the dinosaur *Baryonyx* was able to catch and eat it.

Wealden prints

Wealden fossils include footprints, and burrows made by shrimps and shellfish. This three-toed dinosaur footprint was probably made by *Iguanodon*, when the dinosaur stepped in some soft sand.

Iguanodon

Iguanodon was the first plant-eating dinosaur ever named. Its teeth showed it was a plant-eater.

Unlike flesh-eating dinosaurs – which have sharp, pointed, curved teeth – *Iguanodon* has rather blunt and broad teeth, with long ridges. But did it walk on all fours or on its hind legs?

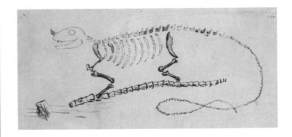

Mantell's drawing

With so few bones to work from, Mantell had no idea what *Iguanodon* looked like. He thought it was a giant lizard that walked on all fours. He even showed it balanced on a branch, as if it was feeding from leaves in the tree. Notice the spiked horn on the nose.

Gideon Mantell

The discoverer of *Iguanodon* was Gideon Mantell (1790–1852), a Sussex doctor, who found its teeth and a few other bones in 1825. It was only the second dinosaur ever named, after *Megalosaurus* (see pp.56–7).

A social animal

Later finds revealed that *Iguanodon* lived in large herds. Skeletons of young and old animals were found in a deep coal mine in Belgium in the 1870s. These also showed for the first time that *Iguanodon* usually walked upright.

Reconstructing *Iguanodon*

After the discoveries in Belgium, the new skeletons were set up for a great display at the Natural History Museum in the capital, Brussels. Each skeleton was carefully wired together, and held up on great metal frameworks. The mystery of Mantell's 'nose horn' was also solved – this was actually a sharp thumb spike. This peaceful plant-eater had a weapon to defend itself!

HYPSILOPHODON

ONE OF THE MOST COMMON OF THE WEALDEN
(SEE P.99) DINOSAURS WAS A SMALL ORNITHOPOD
CALLED *HYPSILOPHODON*. IT WAS NAMED IN
1869, AND DOZENS OF SKELETONS OF THIS
2.3M-LONG PLANT-EATER HAVE BEEN FOUND.

ANATOMY OF THE JAWS

Hypsilophodon had a short snout and rows of peg-like
teeth in its jaws. There was a set of teeth near the front of
the mouth that was used for snipping leaves and fronds,
and a row further back that was used for chewing. As its
jaws moved up and down, its cheek bones moved in and
out by a few millimetres. Most reptiles, then and today,
do not chew their food – they simply swallow it whole.

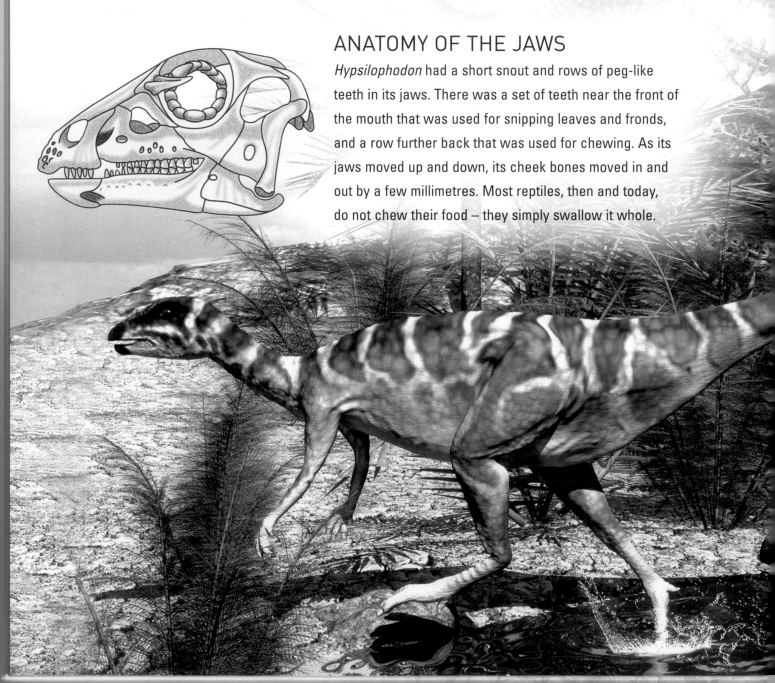

THOMAS HUXLEY

Hypsilophodon was named by Thomas Henry Huxley (1825–95), a great biologist and palaeontologist of Victorian times. Huxley was interested in living and fossil animals, and he wrote many popular books to explain all the new scientific discoveries of the 19th century to ordinary people. He is famous for being one of the first scientists to support Darwin's theory of evolution, and helped establish this revolutionary new idea as the basis of modern biology.

TREE-PERCHER OR RUNNER?

Palaeontologists have debated how *Hypsilophodon* stood and ran. One early idea was that it perched in trees (right), so that it could reach leaves high above the ground. However, this idea is wrong because a percher needs grasping feet, and *Hypsilophodon*'s feet could not grip a branch. So, if it had tried to stand in a tree, it would have fallen out! In fact, *Hypsilophodon* was a fast ground runner (below).

Ornithopods

The ornithopods, such as *Iguanodon* and *Hypsilophodon*, became very important in the Cretaceous.

The group first appeared in the Triassic, and were a minor group in the Jurassic. They replaced the sauropods as major plant-eaters in the Cretaceous.

Evolution and adaptation

Through the 160 million years of their evolution, ornithopods evolved many new features, including remarkable adaptations for plant-eating – their jaws and teeth in particular. The early ornithopods relied on speed rather than armour to escape from predators, so they developed a slender and speedy physique.

Heterodontosaurus

From the Early Jurassic of South Africa, *Heterodontosaurus* could walk on all fours, or run on its hind legs. Its specialized teeth are particularly amazing (see p.35).

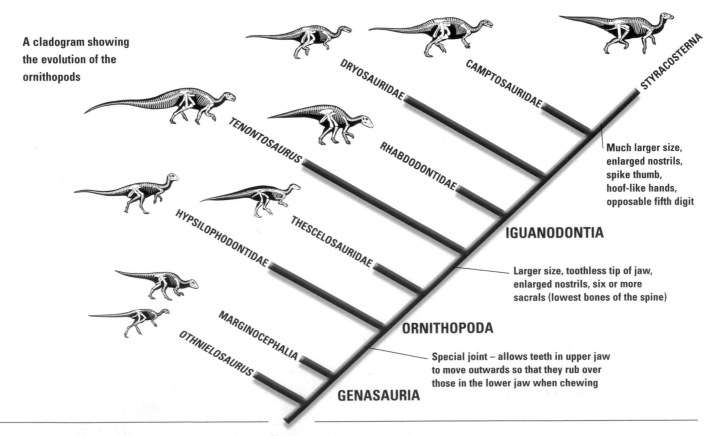

A cladogram showing the evolution of the ornithopods

DRYOSAURIDAE

CAMPTOSAURIDAE

STYRACOSTERNA

TENONTOSAURUS

RHABDODONTIDAE

Much larger size, enlarged nostrils, spike thumb, hoof-like hands, opposable fifth digit

HYPSILOPHODONTIDAE

THESCELOSAURIDAE

IGUANODONTIA

Larger size, toothless tip of jaw, enlarged nostrils, six or more sacrals (lowest bones of the spine)

MARGINOCEPHALIA

ORNITHOPODA

OTHNIELOSAURUS

Special joint – allows teeth in upper jaw to move outwards so that they rub over those in the lower jaw when chewing

GENASAURIA

Tenontosaurus

By the Early Cretaceous, some ornithopods had reached huge sizes. *Tenontosaurus* was up to 8m long. This gave it protection from predators, except when they hunted in packs (see p.121). *Tenontosaurus* was a North American relative of *Iguanodon*.

Early reconstruction of *Iguanodon* in the squatting or 'kangaroo' posture

Posture

Early reconstructions showed ornithopods with the body upright, and the hind legs tucked back. It is now clear that they stood tall, with the legs straighter and the backbone nearly horizontal, so that the weight of the ornithopod's body was balanced by the weight of the tail.

The power of the jaw

The secret to the success of the ornithopods was that they could chew. *Heterodontosaurus* could chew by rotating its lower jaws from side to side. The later, Cretaceous ornithopods chewed by moving their cheek bones in and out, creating side-to-side movements of the back teeth that helped to tear up their tough plant food.

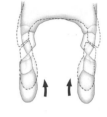

In heterodontosaurs, the lower jaw squeezed in and out as the jaw closed and opened.

In later ornithopods, the upper jaw bone moved in and out as the jaws moved up and down.

This resulted in the up and down jaw movement causing the upper jaw bone to move in and out, producing sideways chewing motions.

Iguanodon's hand and thumb

This ornithopod had hands that could be used for grasping and for walking. Each finger carried a small hoof, rather than a claw, and could stand up to a great deal of wear as the animal walked around. But the thumb was different. It was a single bone – a stout, pointed claw or spike. The thumb spike must have been for defence – a quick way to gouge an attacker.

Liaoning Province

In the last ten years, one area in northeast China has become famous for Early Cretaceous fossil finds.

The Jehol Group of Liaoning Province, and surrounding areas, has produced some of the most amazing fossils ever unearthed. They include dinosaurs with feathers!

Amadeus Grabau

Grabau (1870–1946), a German-American palaeontologist, was one of the first westerners to be allowed to work in China. He was appointed professor at Peking National University, and discovered the rocks and fossils of the Jehol Group.

Fossil rocks

The Jehol Group is mainly in Liaoning Province, but also in Hebei and Inner Mongolia provinces. During the Cretaceous, this area had a warm climate. The rocks were laid down mainly in great freshwater lakes.

Microraptor fossil (see pp.114–15).

Large eye socket shows dinosaur had excellent vision

Fossil find

This skull is 11cm long and belonged to a theropod dinosaur that had distinctive front teeth like those of a rodent. Named *Incisivosaurus* (see p.111), which means 'incisor lizard', it was collected from the lowermost (earliest) levels of the Yixian Formation in western Liaoning.

Excavating fossils

Thousands of fossils have been excavated from the Jehol Group by Chinese palaeontologists. Some of the fossils come out of deep mines, dug out by workers as they follow a particularly fossil-rich rock layer. In other cases, the palaeontologists open a quarry like this one, and work down layer by layer. Some rock beds may have a bird or dinosaur skeleton every metre or so!

Land rich in fossils

The Liaoning landscape's gentle, rolling hills are covered with fields. When the farmers dig for road stone, they find fossils everywhere.

FLOWERS FLOURISH

ONE OF THE MOST REMARKABLE EVENTS WAS THE EVOLUTION OF FLOWERING PLANTS. IN THE EARLY CRETACEOUS, THEY BEGAN TO BECOME ESTABLISHED AROUND THE WORLD. BY THE END OF THE CRETACEOUS, THEY HAD TAKEN OVER.

FOSSIL FINDS

One of the oldest fossil flowers, this specimen of *Archaefructus* comes from the Early Cretaceous of Liaoning Province in China. This flower was found in the same rocks as the remarkable specimens of birds and dinosaurs with feathers (see pp.116–17), but it is not clear whether those dinosaurs ate such plants. The plant-eating dinosaurs preferred ferns and cycads.

ANATOMY OF A FLOWER

The new plant groups of the Cretaceous had flowers, unlike primitive groups such as ferns, cycads and conifers. The flower evolved as a device to spread pollen, either by wind or on the bodies of pollinating animals. The pollen is produced by stamens and is deposited on the carpel in the middle of the flower, where sperm passes down to fertilize the developing seeds. The seeds ripen, the flower withers, and the seeds are then scattered on the ground where many new plants may grow.

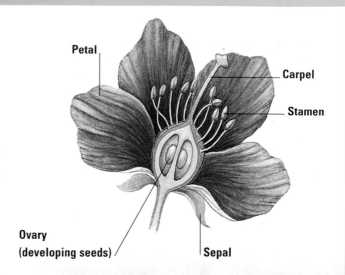

Petal

Carpel

Stamen

Ovary
(developing seeds)

Sepal

TERRESTRIAL REVOLUTION

Flowering plants were small and rare when they first appeared some 120 million years ago. But their new way of breeding, involving flowers and pollination, gave them great advantages — for example, many could survive being eaten by herbivores and produce new plants. Slowly, through the rest of the Cretaceous, flowering plants began to dominate. Their pollinators were insect groups such as bees, ants and termites that fed on the leaves and seeds, and animals that fed on the insects. This remarkable revolution marked the beginning of modern terrestrial ecosystems.

Feathered dinosaurs

The Jehol fossil beds of China give us a remarkable insight into life in the Early Cretaceous. The fossils are of smaller dinosaurs, birds and mammals.

The Jehol rocks were deposited mainly in lakes (see pp.106–7), and preserve beautifully the delicate feathers of birds and dinosaurs.

Sinosauropteryx

This little Jehol dinosaur was one of the first to be found, in 1996. It shocked palaeontologists. Here was a dinosaur, something like *Compsognathus* from the Late Jurassic of Europe (see p.83), but with feathers along its tail and over its back! Did this mean that all, or most, dinosaurs actually had feathers?

Beipiaosaurus

Beipiaosaurus is a therizinosaur, one of a group of strange, plant-eating theropods (see pp.136–7). This medium-sized dinosaur, 2.2m long, had two kinds of feathers – short down feathers and long, filament-like feathers, up to 10cm long, behind its arms.

Dilong

When *Dilong* was named in 2004, it was identified as a primitive tyrannosauroid, an ancestor of *Tyrannosaurus rex*. It had feathers in the jaw and tail regions at the very least. The feathers on the tail formed a tuft at the end, and were probably used for signalling. So, a classic question is, 'Did *Tyrannosaurus rex* have feathers?' The answer is probably 'yes'.

The name *Dilong* means 'emperor dragon', and only one species has been found.

Sinornithosaurus

This was a dromaeosaurid dinosaur, the group that includes *Deinonychus* (see pp.120–1) – probably the closest group to birds. *Sinornithosaurus* had long, bird-like feathers on its arms, yet it could not fly and was a dinosaur. The function of the wings is unknown.

Chinese palaeontologist Xu Xing (see p.115) found and named *Sinornithosaurus*.

Sinovenator

This chicken-sized dinosaur is a troodontid, the group that includes the brainy, slender theropods of the Late Cretaceous (see p.134). Its feathers are not preserved because the fossil was found in coarse river sands rather than the usual fine-grained lake muds.

Incisivosaurus

The Chinese fossils never cease to amaze – but nobody expected to find a goofy dinosaur with big front teeth! *Incisivosaurus*, named in 2002, is a relative of *Oviraptor* (see p.135) and a member of a group of usually toothless theropods. The teeth were not sharp, so perhaps this strange-looking dinosaur was a herbivore. It could have used its front teeth to snatch up tough plant stems.

Caudipteryx

One of the most controversial fossils from the Jehol beds of China is *Caudipteryx*. This specimen reawakened the long debate about whether birds evolved from dinosaurs.

FEATHER EVOLUTION

Feathers developed from protofeathers on compsognathids such as *Sinosauropteryx*.

The first feathers were just bristles that grew from elongated scales.

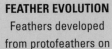

Then the bristles became 'fluffy' as they split into several branches.

Finally, true feathers evolved in *Caudipteryx*, with a central quil.

Birds today have fluffy 'down' feathers that keep their bodies warm.

The vane feathers are used for flight on the wings, and they cover the back and tail.

Sinosauropteryx (see p.110) had short, tufty feathers, but *Caudipteryx* had long feathers on its arms like the flight feathers of modern birds.

Feathered dinosaur

The *Caudipteryx* specimens have long feathers behind the hands. These have a central quill to fix into the skin, and a row of fine branches along the sides.

Evolution debate

The feathered dinosaurs from China clinched the debate over the origin of birds for most people. Birds are dinosaurs, and feathers evolved among the land-living dinosaurs long before birds achieved flight.

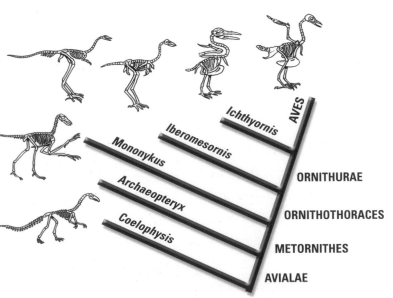

Mononykus · Iberomesornis · Ichthyornis · AVES · Archaeopteryx · Coelophysis · ORNITHURAE · ORNITHOTHORACES · METORNITHES · AVIALAE

Feathery fossil

This photograph shows the arm of *Caudipteryx* and its arm feathers. The clawed hand and arm bones are seen at the top. Extending downwards are blackish impressions of ten or so long feathers. These seem to be rooted in the back of the hand. In life, the feathers passed through the skin and touched the bone, and they may have been moved by tiny muscles at their roots.

MICRORAPTOR

In 2000, while palaeontologists debated the origin of flight and of birds, an astonishing four-winged dinosaur from China was unveiled. Was *Microraptor* a bird or a flying dinosaur? Or could it have been a winged dinosaur that did not fly?

FOSSIL FINDS

The fossils could not be clearer. *Microraptor* is a dromaeosaurid dinosaur and not a bird. And yet it has beautifully preserved sets of flight feathers behind each arm and each leg. The detail in the fossil is so clear that there can be no doubt. However, the wings are not large enough to carry the weight of its body, so *Microraptor* was not able to fly properly.

IN THE FOREST

It has been suggested that *Microraptor* scrambled up tree trunks, and glided from tree to tree, snapping at lizards and dragonflies as it passed. Biologists have long debated whether gliders could become flyers, and this fossil suggests they could. A glider just holds out its wings to stay in the air, while a flyer flaps its wings.

XU XING

Much of the work on the Jehol dinosaurs has been done by the Chinese palaeontologist Xu Xing, born in 1969. Since he described *Sinornithosaurus* and *Beipiaosaurus* in 1999, he has named 30 new dinosaurs from China – the highest total of any living dinosaurologist!

The Chinese birds

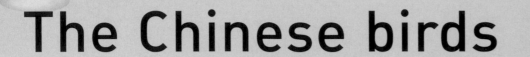

In the past ten years, fossils found in the Jehol rocks have doubled our knowledge of Cretaceous birds.

Until 1990, there was a long gap in the fossil record between the Late Jurassic and the Late Cretaceous. The Jehol birds show the link between *Archaeopteryx* (see pp.84–5) and more modern birds.

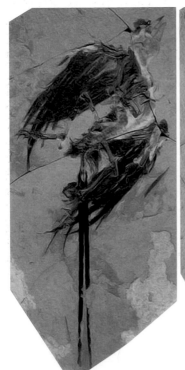

Confuciusornis

Named after the great Chinese philosopher Confucius, this is one of the most common Early Cretaceous birds – more than 2,000 complete specimens have been reported. The female had a short tail, and the male (above) had two streamer-like feathers on the tail that were probably used for displays.

Eoconfuciusornis

The oldest confuciusornithid bird, it was named in 2008. The original specimen (above), is a thin slab of rock split in two, showing both sides of the bird. There are two long tail feathers, and the wing feathers have a striped pattern, perhaps reflecting the colours of the feathers.

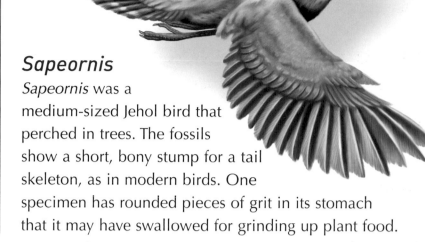

Longipteryx

This pigeon-sized bird was unusual in that it had a long beak, with a group of small teeth at the tip. *Longipteryx* may have been a diving bird that plunged into lakes and rivers, snapping up fishes or small shrimps.

Sapeornis

Sapeornis was a medium-sized Jehol bird that perched in trees. The fossils show a short, bony stump for a tail skeleton, as in modern birds. One specimen has rounded pieces of grit in its stomach that it may have swallowed for grinding up plant food.

Jeholornis

This was the largest bird of the time, about the size of a turkey. Perhaps, like turkeys and chickens, it ran about on the ground, and only flew when it needed to escape from a predator.

Sinornis

This small perching bird shared many primitive features with *Archaeopteryx* in the snout and hindlimbs. However, the shape of its wings is more advanced and better adapted for flight.

EARTH EVIDENCE

DOUBLE FOSSIL LAKE FINDS

The Jehol bird specimens are amazing, and many thousands have been found since 1995. Some, like this fossil of two *Confuciusornis* (left), contain two skeletons – the drawing on the right shows them clearly. The rock is a fine muddy limestone, laid down in a warm, shallow lake, and it is still a puzzle why so many birds became trapped. Perhaps some of them were dipping in the surface of the water to snatch fish or other pieces of food, and became waterlogged and sank.

Ceratopsians

The ceratopsians were a Cretaceous dinosaur group, famous for the face horns and great frills seen in later forms. The first ceratopsians were small and lacked horns.

Psittacosaurus meileyingensis from China had a short snout and neck frill.

Psittacosaurus neimongoliensis, also from China, had a narrower snout.

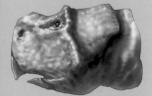

Psittacosaurus sibiricus, found in Russia, was the largest known species of them all.

Psittacosaurus and *Protoceratops* from the Early Cretaceous of China and Mongolia were first discovered in the 1920s. Since then, hundreds of specimens have been excavated all over eastern Asia. These were the sheep of their day!

Fossil nest

The discovery in 2004 of an adult *Psittacosaurus* with 34 babies was a surprise. The adult is 2m long, and the juveniles some 50cm long. This suggests they had not just hatched from the eggs – at birth, they would have been half that length or less. So is this a real fossil, or have the specimens been washed together somehow?

Modelling the nest

Most palaeontologists accept that the adult is probably the mother or father of most of the young, and the juveniles might be a year or more old. Perhaps they huddled together for protection from an approaching storm. They are preserved in volcanic ash, so it is possible a nearby volcano erupted, and the hot ash formed their tomb.

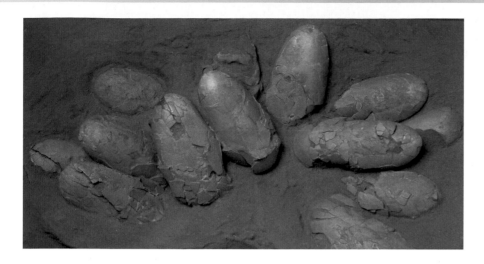

The wrong eggs

When nests of these long eggs were found in the 1920s, they were identified as those of the ceratopsian *Protoceratops*. This early ceratopsian mother supposedly laid her eggs in circles in shallow hollows scraped in sand, and stayed around to protect her young.

Nests in danger

Many paintings have been made to show this scene (right). Menaced by the fearsome theropod *Oviraptor* – its name means 'egg thief' – the mother *Protoceratops* stands her ground. The skeletons of *Oviraptor* were found near the nests with eggs, and palaeontologists thought that they had found a scene of hunting preserved for 100 million years. But nobody thought to look inside the eggs.

Not guilty!

In fact, the eggs belonged to *Oviraptor*. When palaeontologists X-rayed them and removed the shells, they found tiny *Oviraptor* babies inside some of them. Two more amazing fossil nests from China and Mongolia have also preserved a mother *Oviraptor* sitting over her eggs, with her feathered arms spread over the nest, apparently protecting it.

The Cloverly Formation

Not many dinosaurs are known from the Early Cretaceous of North America, but the Cloverly Formation in Wyoming has revealed some, after excavations during the 1960s.

John Ostrom and his team had heard of bones in the Cloverly Formation, and they set up field camps. In 1964, they found complete skeletons of *Deinonychus*, an efficient theropod hunter.

Deinonychus

For years, there had been a mystery about dromaeosaurid dinosaurs. Some isolated toe bones and skull remains had been found in Canada and the USA in the 1920s, and named *Dromaeosaurus*. The 1964 discoveries showed the whole animal, and Ostrom was able to present a very detailed account of its astonishing anatomy.

Razor claw

Most striking was the slashing claw on the second toe of the foot. When it ran, *Deinonychus* kept the claw folded back. To attack, it moved the claw down fast in an arc-shaped movement, damaging its prey.

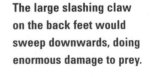

The large slashing claw on the back feet would sweep downwards, doing enormous damage to prey.

Deinonychus and birds

Ostrom's work on *Deinonychus* showed dromaeosaurids are close relatives of birds. Ostrom showed that every bone in *Deinonychus* was nearly the same as those in the first bird, *Archaeopteryx* (see pp.84–5).

Hunting as a pack

Deinonychus was only 3.4m long, but its main prey, *Tenontosaurus* (see p.105), was more than twice the length, and four or five times the weight. Ostrom guessed that this smart predator hunted in packs, and in 1995 he reported a new excavation site where a dead *Tenontosaurus* was surrounded by some dead *Deinonychus* and scattered teeth.

The Bighorn Basin

Many dinosaur sites in North America are in 'badlands', so called because they are 'bad lands' for farming and people. But these open, desert-like areas are 'good lands' for dinosaurs – palaeontologists can spot bones in the rapidly eroding gullies. The Bighorn Basin, Wyoming, is 130km across and includes the Cloverly Formation.

John Ostrom

Professor of palaeontology at Yale University, John Ostrom (1928–2005) worked first on hadrosaurs, and then began excavations in the Cloverly Formation. His discovery of *Deinonychus* led to a complete revolution in modern palaeontological thought. He showed that birds evolved from dinosaurs, and that many dinosaurs, including *Deinonychus*, were warm-blooded.

AFRICAN DINOSAURS

IN THE LAST 100 YEARS, THERE HAVE BEEN SPECTACULAR FOSSIL FINDS IN NORTHERN AFRICA, MANY OF THEM DATING FROM THE EARLY CRETACEOUS, 110 MYA.

OURANOSAURUS

Herds of this duck-billed iguanodont once wandered across the swampy plains of northwest Africa. *Ouranosaurus* was a herbivore, with large groups, or batteries, of teeth on the sides of its jaws to crush and chew plants. These dinosaurs had a spiny ridge along their back, which they may have used to absorb heat from the sun.

NORTH AFRICA

● **Main fossil sites**

In North Africa, there were German expeditions to Egypt and French ones to Morocco and the Niger Republic during the 20th century. In the 1990s, US expeditions not only found more fossils of known species, but also discovered new dinosaurs.

JOBARIA

This sauropod was named after 'Jobar', a creature that appears in local legends. Its fossils were found in what is now the Sahara desert. It was about 18m long and could rear up on its hind legs to reach its plant food. Its backbone and tail are very simple when compared with the complex ones of the North American sauropods, such as *Apatosaurus* and *Diplodocus*.

SARCOSUCHUS

One of the largest crocodilians to have walked the Earth, *Sarcosuchus* weighed about 10 tonnes and was up to 12m in length, with a skull as big as a human adult's body. It prowled the river banks, crushing fish and larger prey – such as *Ouranosaurus* – with the 132 teeth in its fearsome jaws.

The crested spinosaurs

Most dinosaurs lived more or less worldwide, but one group lived mainly in Africa – the spinosaurs. The name refers to the long spines on their backs.

The first spinosaurs were found one hundred years ago in Egypt. Their teeth and bones are found in all the countries of North Africa, on the fringes of the Sahara desert.

Baryonyx

One spinosaur skeleton was found in England, and this helped palaeontologists to understand the group better. *Baryonyx* is known from a complete skeleton that had spines down its back and a long-snouted, crocodile-like skull. The jaws seem weak, so perhaps these dinosaurs were fish-eaters.

Ernst Stromer

Ernst Stromer (1870–1952) found the first spinosaur, *Spinosaurus*, in Egypt, and named it in 1912. He brought this and many other dinosaurs back to Munich in Germany. Sadly, the museum was bombed in 1944, and the entire collection was lost, apart from his journals and the published description and drawings of *Spinosaurus*.

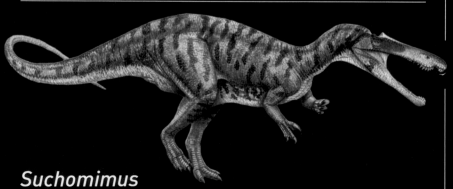

Suchomimus

In 1998, Paul Sereno and his team found *Suchomimus*, 'crocodile mimic', in Niger, just south of the Sahara desert. This 11m-long African spinosaur was very like *Baryonyx*. It had the same crocodile-like skull.

Assembling a skeleton

Paul Sereno puts the finishing touches to a museum mount of his discovery, *Suchomimus*. This new find is a good example of the anatomy of spinosaurs. In life, the long spines down the backbone supported a low crest – the spines were longer and the crest higher in *Spinosaurus*.

Polar dinosaurs

Surely dinosaurs could not live in the freezing snows of the north or south poles – or could they?

In the Cretaceous, Australia lay closer to the south pole. South Australia, where dinosaurs have been found, was in icy cold latitudes.

Dinosaur Cove

One site in Victoria, on the south coast of Australia, has produced many dinosaur bones and is called Dinosaur Cove. The rocks are Early Cretaceous, from about 106 mya, younger than the Jehol Group of China (see pp.106–7) and the Cloverly Formation of North America (see pp.120–1).

In the field

Dinosaur Cove was a tough place to work. The bones were buried in hard rock that had to be drilled out, so the team dug caves into the cliffs. They even had to use explosives.

Leaellynasaura and **Timimus** wander along beside the lake in Dinosaur Cove.

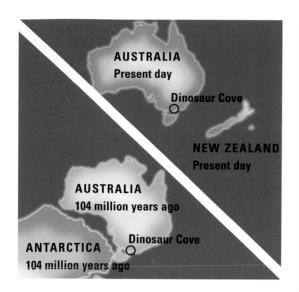

AUSTRALIA
Present day

Dinosaur Cove

NEW ZEALAND
Present day

AUSTRALIA
104 million years ago

ANTARCTICA
104 million years ago

Dinosaur Cove

Near the pole

This geographic reconstruction shows that, during the Cretaceous, Australia was breaking free from Antarctica as Gondwana broke up. Parts of Australia lay within the Antarctic circle, and Dinosaur Cove was close to the south pole. Lakes and rivers would have frozen in winter. The dinosaurs must have migrated north to find food.

Atlascopcosaurus

This small plant-eater is a relative of *Hypsilophodon* from England (see pp.102–3). *Atlascopcosaurus* was 2–3m long, but it is known only from a few fragments of the skull and skeleton, so this reconstruction is based on its close relatives.

Timimus

There are not many large predators in the Dinosaur Cove deposits. Some isolated leg bones show that *Timimus* was probably an ornithomimid, a member of a group that became more widespread in the Late Cretaceous.

Leaellynasaura

This small hypsilophodontid is named after Leaellyn, the daughter of Tom and Patricia Vickers-Rich, who discovered it. *Leaellynasaura* was less than 1m long and fed on the ferns and cycads found at the same site.

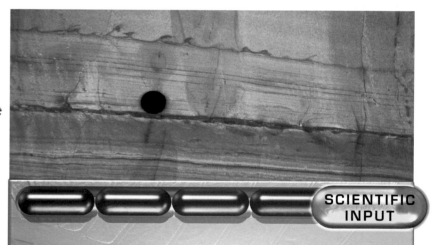

SCIENTIFIC INPUT

EVIDENCE FOR ICE

Evidence of ice in the Dinosaur Cove rocks comes from plants. The plant remains show very narrow growth rings because they stopped growing each year during winter. The rocks also show evidence. This vertical section of finely-banded mud has 'flame structures', where the damp mud was frozen in winter, and then melted and became fluid. The weight of sediment above forced the fluid to escape upwards in narrow tubes.

Dinosaur facts

The world of the dinosaurs was full of many plants and animals that no longer exist because they have become extinct. However, there were many other plants and animals that lived during the Mesozoic that we would find familiar today.

PLANTS

- Mosses – low green moss covered the rocks and trees.
- Ferns – fern fronds filled dark nooks and crannies.
- Tree ferns – dinosaurs loved to eat tree ferns, but they are not as common today.
- Conifer trees – many dinosaurs fed on the needles and broader leaves of ancestors of the pines and the monkey puzzle.
- Flowering plants – dinosaurs did not eat grass, cabbages or flowers, but the first flowering plants, such as magnolia and roses, appeared in the middle of the Cretaceous.

ANIMALS

- Worms – earthworms churned the soil.
- Snails – slugs and snails lived among the dead leaves and fed on plants.
- Beetles – bugs, cockroaches and beetles lived on trees and under leaves.
- Ants and termites – in the Cretaceous, these colony-living insects appeared after the evolution of flowering plants.
- Bees and wasps – these honey-gatherers appeared in the Cretaceous.
- Butterflies and moths – these insects fed on nectar from Cretaceous flowers.
- Fishes – modern-style fishes lived in the sea, and in rivers and lakes.
- Frogs and salamanders – these amphibians appeared in the Triassic, becoming common in the Cretaceous.
- Lizards – the first lizards are Jurassic, and many modern groups appeared in the Cretaceous.
- Snakes – the first snakes appeared in the Cretaceous.
- Turtles – these animals swam in ponds and crept about on the land from the Late Triassic onwards.
- Crocodiles – these fish-eaters lived in ponds and seas from the Jurassic.
- Birds – *Archaeopteryx* appeared in the Late Jurassic and birds became very varied in the Cretaceous.
- Mammals – the first mammals of the Triassic gave rise to some modern-style mammals in the Cretaceous.

The fossil skeleton of a *Dromaeosaur* about to attack its prey

WEBSITES ON LIFE DURING THE MESOZOIC ERA

www.ucmp.berkeley.edu/mesozoic/mesozoic.html   A guide to the main groups of life in the Mesozoic.

www.livescience.com/38596-mesozoic-era.html   An in-depth look at climate and life in the Mesozoic.

http://palaeo.gly.bris.ac.uk/macro/supertree/KTR.html   How flora and fauna changed in the Cretaceous.

www.fossilmuseum.net/Paleobiology/Mesozoic_Paleobiology.htm   Lots of Mesozoic fossils.

CHANGE
AND EXTINCTION

The Late Cretaceous saw the continents continue to move apart.

Dinosaurs in different parts of the world evolved to become

different from each other. New groups, such as hadrosaurs,

ceratopsians and ankylosaurs became common. But it all ended

65 million years ago when a massive meteorite hit the Earth,

killing the dinosaurs and many other forms of life.

Mongolian expeditions

When the first fossils were found in Mongolia, northern China, in the 1920s, they caused a sensation.

The first expedition was from New York City in search of early human fossils. Instead, they found an amazing haul of dinosaur skeletons.

Roy Chapman Andrews

Chapman Andrews (1884–1960) was hired by the American Museum of Natural History to lead the expeditions to Mongolia. He had already toured the world, including China, collecting specimens for the museum, and he was used to the difficult conditions he would meet in the desert.

The 1923 expedition

Altogether, Chapman Andrews led six US expeditions between 1922 and 1930. In 1923, the team found complete skeletons of *Psittacosaurus* and *Protoceratops* (see pp.118–19) and the theropod *Oviraptor*. This was the expedition that recovered complete nests, which caused a sensation when they were exhibited.

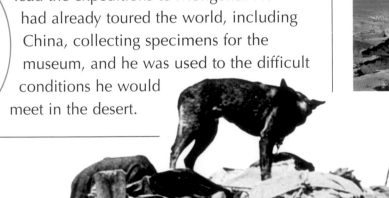

The sands of the Gobi desert are a hostile environment in which to hunt for dinosaurs.

Velociraptor

Another of the 1923 finds was *Velociraptor*, an extraordinary little theropod. Its name means 'speedy hunter'. This 1m-long predator is now known to be a close relative of *Deinonychus* (see p.121).

Mongolia

In the Cretaceous, Mongolia was not desert, but a rich and fertile habitat for dinosaurs. The area lay further north than it does today, and was covered with rivers and great lakes full of fish and other life. The watersides were lined with plants that provided a rich diet for dinosaurs.

Velociraptor's skull

The scientists were amazed by the lightweight skull armed with vicious teeth. It probably fed on mammals, lizards and other smaller animals.

Members of the 1925 expedition push their vehicles through the sand.

AMAZING FACTS

FIGHT TO THE DEATH

This amazing fossil, discovered in 1971, is of a juvenile *Velociraptor* (left) attacking a *Protoceratops* (right), which bit down on the predator's right hand with its beak-like jaws. *Velociraptor*'s hind claw is embedded in the belly of the *Protoceratops*. Palaeontologists have debated how this fight scene was preserved. The struggling dinosaurs may have been overcome by a sandstorm that killed them instantly.

The Nemegt Formation

The Nemegt Formation is the source of 25 dinosaurs, including the pachycephalosaur *Homalocephale*, the sauropod *Nemegtosaurus* and the theropod *Tarbosaurus*.

The formation was discovered by US expeditions in the 1920s, but it was excavated thoroughly by expeditions from the Soviet Union in the 1950s. The Soviets used bulldozers to excavate skeletons of the giant theropod *Tarbosaurus* (see pp.134–5). Expeditions from Poland in the 1960s unearthed *Nemegtosaurus*.

Fossil finds

A Mongolian boy proudly holds up the thigh bone of *Nemegtosaurus*, the sauropod. Many of the fossils from Mongolia are in excellent condition, and complete, like this specimen. Since 1960, palaeontologists have trained in Mongolia, and much of the work is done by these scientists, working with overseas collaborators from the USA, Japan and Europe.

The first task is to protect the fossil bones with a covering of paper or foil.

Plaster powder is mixed with water to make a paste, which is smeared on to bandages.

The bandages of sacking, or burlap, in plaster are smoothed over the bones.

The bandaged block is allowed to dry, and then is turned over. Wooden planks are plastered onto the base to strengthen the block.

Excavating fossil bones

Dinosaur bones may seem big and tough, but they are actually fragile. Since the early days, palaeontologists have used bandages in plaster to strengthen the specimens – the process is the same as when doctors bandage a broken leg. The plaster protects the bones while they are in transit. It is cut off in the lab and the bones can then be carefully removed from the rock.

Nemegt expedition

A line of 11 trucks sets out across the wild plains of Mongolia to excavate giant dinosaurs in the Nemegt Formation. Expeditions to such remote areas often have to be large – the palaeontologists must carry all their equipment with them, including enough food, water and fuel for a month or more.

Flesh-eaters of Mongolia

Late Cretaceous theropods were amazingly diverse in size and shape, more so than at any time before.

Some smaller theropods became very fast and brainy. Others became massive and powerful enough to attack the largest plant-eaters.

Gallimimus

This ornithomimid belonged to one of several theropod groups that lost their teeth. It had a sharp-edged beak to snap at prey. At one time, people thought that ornithomimids were egg-eaters.

Saurornithoides

The troodontids were slender and fast-moving dinosaurs. *Saurornithoides* was 3m long and almost certainly covered in feathers. It had good eyesight and a large brain, probably to help it hunt fast-moving lizards and mammals.

Saurornithoides had long-fingered hands for snatching prey.

Tarbosaurus' skull

This skull was high and narrow. The height meant that *Tarbosaurus* could have powerful jaw muscles to drive its teeth deep into prey.

The massive hindlimbs had large, three-toed feet for holding down the prey.

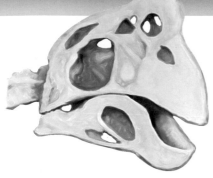

Finds from China show that *Oviraptor* was covered in feathers.

Oviraptor's skull

One of the weirdest toothless theropods was *Oviraptor*, with its high, short snout. The skull is very lightweight, with enormous openings and thin, bony struts. This design allowed the animal to move quickly.

Oviraptor

This is one of the astonishing dinosaurs discovered during the US expeditions to Mongolia in the 1920s (see pp.130–1). The strangely-shaped skull may have been brightly coloured in life, as a signalling device.

EARTH
EVIDENCE

Tarbosaurus

The first skeletons of *Tarbosaurus* were excavated in the 1950s, in the Nemegt Formation (see pp.132–3). The dinosaur was a close relative of *Tyrannosaurus* from North America (see pp.144–5), but there are differences in the skull.

PERFECT FOSSILS

The skeletons of *Tarbosaurus* were extraordinary when they were found, in the 1950s, because they were more or less complete. The Soviet palaeontologists had to drive massive trucks and bulldozers to the Nemegt, and they even used explosives to speed up the process of extracting the fossil skeletons. These were transported back to Russia by truck and train, and they may now be seen on show in Moscow.

THERIZINOSAURS

THE THERIZINOSAURS HAVE BEEN A REAL MYSTERY THAT HAS ONLY JUST BEEN SOLVED. THE FIRST SPECIMENS FOUND BY THE SOVIETS IN MONGOLIA IN THE 1950S WERE THOUGHT TO BE THE REMAINS OF TURTLES, THEROPODS AND SAUROPODOMORPHS.

THERIZINOSAURUS

When Soviet palaeontologists dug up a number of massive, 1m-long scythe-like claws, they thought – perhaps surprisingly – that these came from a giant turtle. The dinosaur was named by Evgeny Maleev in 1954 and other bones came to light in the following years. It was only in 1993, when complete skeletons of its close relative, *Alxasaurus,* were found in China, that *Therizinosaurus* was identified as a dinosaur.

Deinocheirus

ARMS AND CLAWS

The most puzzling of the Mongolian fossils belonged to a dinosaur that was named *Deinocheirus* in 1970. This pair of huge arms (above right) with claws of about 20–30cm in length might come from a therizinosaur, or maybe from a huge ornithomimosaur, a distant relative of *Gallimimus* (see p.134). Either way, the function of such long and powerful arms, armed with terrifying claws, remains a mystery.

Segnosaurus

SKULL

SKULL AND HIPS

The skulls of therizinosaurs have tiny teeth, so palaeontologists realized that the animal must have been a plant-eater. They decided it was a sauropodomorph or ornithischian, or even something in between. The hip bones were not much help because they have the pubis and ischium running parallel, which is an ornithischian feature (see pp.26–7). However, the discovery of complete skeletons shows that the therizinosaurs were not only theropods but plant-eaters as well.

Ilium

Ischium

Pubis

HIP BONES

Hadrosaurs

In the Late Cretaceous, some of the most common dinosaurs were the hadrosaurs, or 'duck-billed dinosaurs', close relatives of ornithopods such as *Iguanodon* (see pp.100–1).

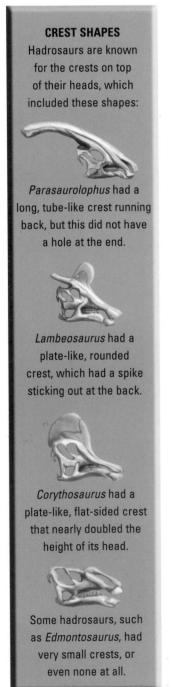

CREST SHAPES
Hadrosaurs are known for the crests on top of their heads, which included these shapes:

Parasaurolophus had a long, tube-like crest running back, but this did not have a hole at the end.

Lambeosaurus had a plate-like, rounded crest, which had a spike sticking out at the back.

Corythosaurus had a plate-like, flat-sided crest that nearly doubled the height of its head.

Some hadrosaurs, such as *Edmontosaurus*, had very small crests, or even none at all.

Hadrosaurs were enormously successful because they had a highly efficient feeding mechanism. There were many successful species in the Late Cretaceous because they apparently used sight and sound to identify their mates.

Anatomy

Hadrosaurs all had very similar skeletons, and these were very like other ornithopods. The head was horse-shaped, and the hind legs were powerful. The arms could be raised from the ground when the animal ran, or they could be used for walking. The hands and feet had small, hoof-like claws and thick sole pads.

Making sounds

When palaeontologists looked inside the head crests of the hadrosaurs, they found the nostrils ran up inside the crests. When the animal breathed, the air whistled through these tubes. Different crest shapes produced different hooting and honking sounds.

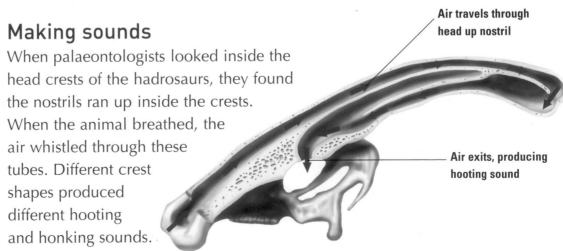

Air travels through head up nostril

Air exits, producing hooting sound

Living in a herd

Many hadrosaur fossils have been found in large numbers, sometimes dozens of skeletons in one site. These 'assemblages' suggest that the hadrosaurs lived in herds. Great herds of hadrosaurs, even several species together, may have fed peacefully side by side, not unlike herds of antelope in Africa today.

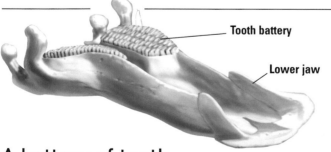

Tooth battery

Lower jaw

A battery of teeth

Some hadrosaurs had 2,000 teeth! There were up to 500 in each side of the lower and upper jaws. The teeth were arranged in rows because they wore out fast. New teeth were lined up, ready to move into place as the top teeth in a series became worn down.

Hatching out

Some hadrosaur eggs have been found with unhatched babies inside. When the eggs are scanned, all the tiny bones can be seen. This model shows that, just before hatching, this baby hadrosaur filled the egg, with its tail wrapped round its body. The baby had a short skull and huge eyes, just like a human baby.

The Romanian islands

Late Cretaceous dinosaurs are not found in parts of Europe because most of the area was under ocean.

However, there were some islands in the south of France and Spain, and in eastern Europe, where Romania is today. Some very strange little dinosaurs have been found in these areas.

The Hateg

The Hateg area of Romania used to be made up of islands. This wild, wooded country with strange, dark castles, was the setting for the story of Dracula, but the Late Cretaceous rocks there are famous for their dinosaur fossils. Today, the area is a dinosaur geopark.

Magyarosaurus

This sauropod was named in 1932, and was only 6m in length – small compared to the closely related titanosaurs, which were 12m or longer. Palaeontologists realized this was a 'dwarf species' – it was smaller than its relatives because it lived on an island.

Telmatosaurus

This ornithopod was also a dwarf dinosaur, some 4m long, compared to typical lengths of 7–10m for its close relatives. It was also the most primitive hadrosaur (see pp.138–9). This suggests that the Hateg dinosaurs had been isolated on the island, evolving slowly compared to their relatives in North America and Asia.

Rhabdodon

Rhabdodon was an unusual, late-surviving iguanodont, related to *Iguanodon* from the Early Cretaceous (see pp.100–1). This dinosaur is known also from the Late Cretaceous islands of southern France. This suggests that these rather primitive dinosaurs were able to survive on small islands.

Baron Franz Nopcsa

Franz Nopcsa (1877–1933) was born of a noble family on the borders of Romania and Hungary. He found fossils on his family estates at Hateg, and named many of the dinosaurs, realizing that they were 'island dwarfs'.

Struthiosaurus

The last Hateg dinosaur is an ankylosaur, up to 2.5m long. *Struthiosaurus* is known from several European islands, in Romania, Austria and France, and it seems to have been more like the Early Cretaceous ankylosaurs from elsewhere.

Struthiosaurus seems to have been a primitive form of ankylosaur.

Argentinian finds

Until recently, not very much was known about the dinosaurs of South America – because not many palaeontologists had even looked for them.

Over the past 20 years, dozens of remarkable new Cretaceous dinosaurs have been reported, especially from Argentina. These specimens show that dinosaurs evolved unique forms on the South American continent.

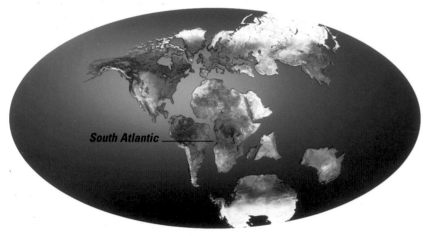

South Atlantic

The Late Cretaceous

The Late Cretaceous world was beginning to look a little like today's. The southern Atlantic Ocean had opened up between South America and Africa, and the old continent of Gondwana was breaking up, as India headed for Asia, and Antarctica and Australia began to separate.

Saltasaurus

One unusual South American group was the titanosaurian sauropods. Sauropods were largely replaced by ornithopods at the beginning of the Cretaceous (see pp.98–9), yet sauropods remained important in South America. Titanosaurs such as *Saltasaurus* had bodies covered in a dense matting of armour plates. The plates provided some protection from attack, but they were not as tough as the armour of the ankylosaurs (see p.149).

Each armour plate was surrounded by many smaller ones.

Saltasaurus nest site

In 1997, Argentinian palaeontologist Luis Chiappe found an amazing dinosaur nesting-ground at Auca Mahuevo in Argentina. There were hundreds of nest mounds over a large area. Some of these carried small eggs, only 11–12cm across. Inside some of the eggs were embryos of unhatched babies, showing pieces of microscopic armour from the skin.

Alvarezsaurus

This small theropod was named in 1991 on the basis of an incomplete skeleton. About 2m long, the animal was slender and lightweight. Close relatives have also been found in Mongolia, and *Alvarezsaurus* is probably closely related to the dinosaur ancestors of birds.

Saltasaurus had a small head on an elongated neck.

Abelisaurus

The great predator of the Argentinian Late Cretaceous was *Abelisaurus*. It was up to 9m long, similar in size to many tyrannosaurs. But *Abelisaurus* belongs to another theropod group, which all had rather high skulls, often with crests above the eyes. The abelisaurids also lived in India and Africa, as well as Madagascar.

TYRANNOSAURS

THE MOST FEARSOME AND FAMOUS DINOSAURS ARE THE TYRANNOSAURS. THESE HUGE HUNTERS, INCLUDING THE 7-TONNE *TYRANNOSAURUS REX*, WERE THE TOP PREDATORS THROUGHOUT THE WORLD IN THE LATE CRETACEOUS.

FOSSIL FIND

This skeleton of *Albertosaurus* shows the key features of the tyrannosaurs: a deep and narrow skull, massive lower jaw, long teeth, quite small forearms with only two or three fingers, a long tail for balance, and massive hindlimbs with great, three-toed feet. Complete skeletons of tyrannosaurs are rare – more often, isolated teeth are found.

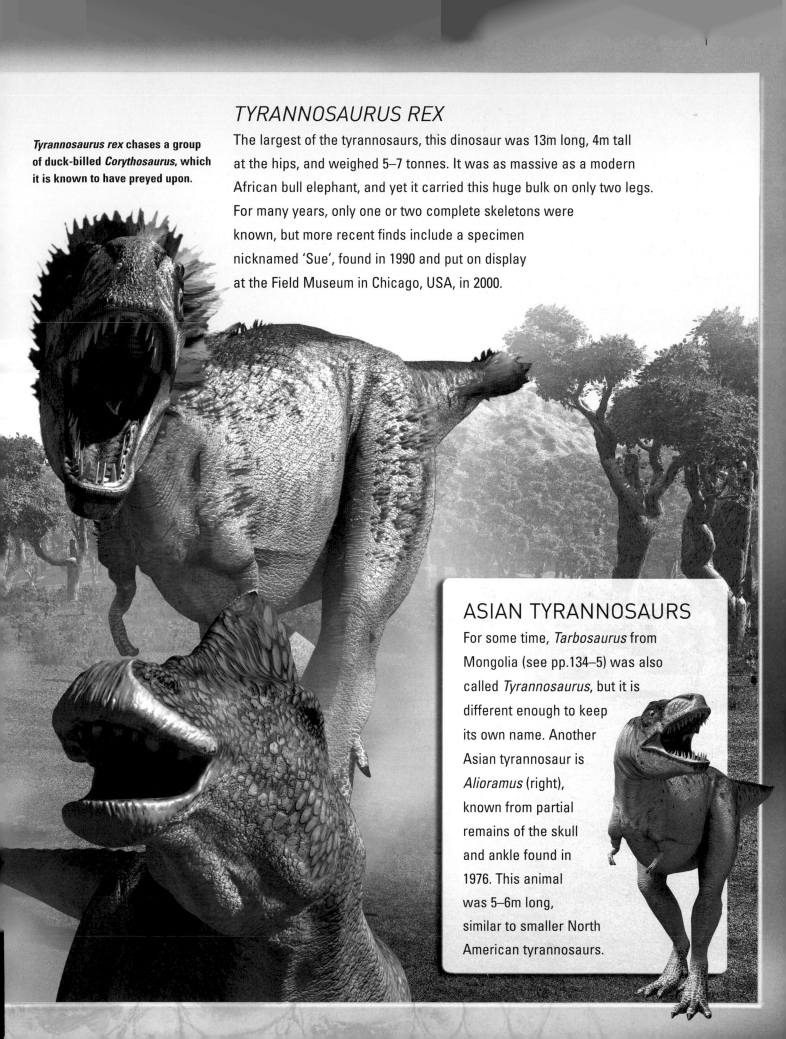

TYRANNOSAURUS REX

The largest of the tyrannosaurs, this dinosaur was 13m long, 4m tall at the hips, and weighed 5–7 tonnes. It was as massive as a modern African bull elephant, and yet it carried this huge bulk on only two legs. For many years, only one or two complete skeletons were known, but more recent finds include a specimen nicknamed 'Sue', found in 1990 and put on display at the Field Museum in Chicago, USA, in 2000.

Tyrannosaurus rex chases a group of duck-billed *Corythosaurus*, which it is known to have preyed upon.

ASIAN TYRANNOSAURS

For some time, *Tarbosaurus* from Mongolia (see pp.134–5) was also called *Tyrannosaurus*, but it is different enough to keep its own name. Another Asian tyrannosaur is *Alioramus* (right), known from partial remains of the skull and ankle found in 1976. This animal was 5–6m long, similar to smaller North American tyrannosaurs.

Triceratops

The ceratopsians were plant-eating dinosaurs of the Late Cretaceous. Their massive heads, armed with spikes and horns, protected them from predators.

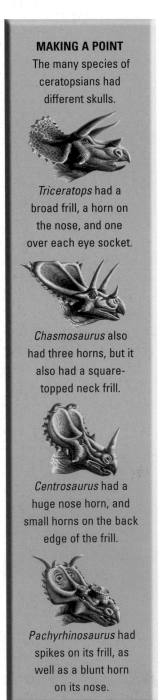

MAKING A POINT

The many species of ceratopsians had different skulls.

Triceratops had a broad frill, a horn on the nose, and one over each eye socket.

Chasmosaurus also had three horns, but it also had a square-topped neck frill.

Centrosaurus had a huge nose horn, and small horns on the back edge of the frill.

Pachyrhinosaurus had spikes on its frill, as well as a blunt horn on its nose.

Triceratops, the best-known ceratopsian, was one of the last to appear before the dinosaur world ended.

Weapons for fighting

The horns may have been partly to fight off meat-eating dinosaurs, but ceratopsians probably tussled with each other. Today, deer and antelope wrestle like this when they are competing for mates.

Armoured dinosaur

The horns of *Triceratops* were a potent weapon against enemies and rivals, but the neck shield has been harder to understand. The shield is made from bone and so weighed a lot. Yet it only protected a short stretch of neck.

Defending young

Ceratopsians lived in herds. Often, fossils of dozens of animals, young and old, are found together. Perhaps, if they were threatened, the adults would form a ring around the young, with their horns pointing outwards. Musk oxen do this today.

Built like a tank

Triceratops was built like a rhinoceros, but it was much larger – 8m long, compared to a 3.5m rhinoceros. The dinosaur had a powerful neck and strong limbs to allow it to carry its huge head, and all the muscles were at the front of the body so it could charge at its attacker. The beak and small teeth were designed for snipping up tough plants.

The last dinosaurs

Once it was thought the dinosaurs drifted slowly to extinction, at the end of the Late Cretaceous.

However, dinosaurs were diverse and abundant right to the end. There is no sign that their days were numbered, and this suggests they may have been killed by something out of the ordinary.

Henry Fairfield Osborn

Osborn (1857–1935) was a director of the American Museum of Natural History in New York City. He sent out the expeditions to Mongolia (see pp.130–1). Teams of AMNH collectors also found the first remains of *Tyrannosaurus rex*, which Osborn named in 1905.

Tyrannosaurus rex

Specimens of *Tyrannosaurus rex* have been found at various levels of rocks in the Late Cretaceous, and some specimens occur right below the KT boundary (see p.149). This giant flesh-eater had to be large to prey on the giant hadrosaur *Edmontosaurus* and the well-defended *Ankylosaurus*.

Edmontosaurus

Many hadrosaurs lived right at the end of the Cretaceous, two species of *Edmontosaurus* among them. This 13m-long dinosaur was one of the largest hadrosaurs, and it is known especially from Canada (it is named after Edmonton, the capital of Alberta). Some specimens even preserve impressions of the skin and gut contents – it fed on ferns and the needles of conifers.

Hell Creek

The Hell Creek Formation is one of the best-known Late Cretaceous rock units that yields dinosaurs. It is across several US states – North Dakota, South Dakota, Montana, Colorado and Wyoming. The rocks were laid down in ancient rivers towards the end of the Cretaceous.

Ankylosaurus

One of the best known of the armoured dinosaurs, *Ankylosaurus* was 7m or more in length, and armed with a great, bony club on its tail. Its whole body was encased in a network of armour plates made from blobs of bone, and it even had a bony eyelid to protect each eye!

EARTH EVIDENCE

Struthiomimus

Struthiomimus was a fast-running predator, related to *Gallimimus* from Mongolia (see p.134). It was more than 4m long, and probably ran like an ostrich. It would have had to dodge predators, and hunt its quick-moving lizard and mammal prey.

THE KT BOUNDARY

A line can be drawn in the rocks of the Hell Creek Formation, and many others of the same age. This line marks the end of the very last dinosaur. Other groups – such as fishes, frogs, lizards, snakes, turtles, crocodiles, birds and mammals – carried on through the boundary. Below the line is Cretaceous, and above the line is Tertiary, and the abbreviation KT means Cretaceous–Tertiary ('K' is used by scientists for Cretaceous, because 'C' is already used for the older Carboniferous era).

IMPACT!

FOR YEARS, SCIENTISTS HAVE DEBATED THE END OF THE DINOSAURS 65 MYA. SEA REPTILES, PTEROSAURS, AMMONITES, BELEMNITES AND MANY OTHER CREATURES BECAME EXTINCT AT EXACTLY THE SAME TIME. MANY THEORIES HAVE BEEN TESTED AND REJECTED. THE CURRENT PREFERRED THEORY, SUPPORTED BY A HUGE AMOUNT OF EVIDENCE, IS THAT THE EARTH WAS HIT BY A MASSIVE METEORITE.

HOW THE WORLD CHANGED

An unusual clay layer marks the end of the Cretaceous. This clay layer shows four steps in the disaster. First, the meteorite hit the Earth and melted the rock, sending small beads of melted glass flying through the air and landing over huge areas. Second, because the meteorite hit sea water in the Caribbean, a huge tsunami, or killer wave, hit the shores. Third, a wave of heated air shot across the Earth causing wildfires. Finally, fine dust fell from high in the air to blanket the Earth.

1. Melted glass beads arrive through the air.

2. A tsunami hits the shore and churns beach rocks.

3. A hot shock wave through the air causes wildfire.

4. Fine dust descends from high in the atmosphere.

THE METEORITE HITS

The meteorite was at least 16km across and it delivered an explosive force at least two million times more powerful than the largest ever atomic bomb. It punched deep into the Earth's crust and produced a huge crater. The force of the impact meant that the meteorite itself was reduced to dust – and this dust, together with millions of tonnes of rock, was thrown out of the crater.

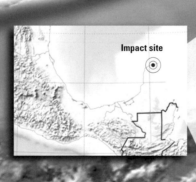

Impact site

CHICXULUB CRATER

For a long time, there was no crater – but the geological evidence for impact was strong. The crater was found in the Yucatán region of Mexico in 1990, buried beneath younger rocks. Geophysical surveys show that the buried crater, some 180km across, is in rocks that once lay beneath the ancient Caribbean sea. Holes drilled through the centre of the crater hit melted rock – and this confirms exactly what had happened.

After the dinosaurs

When the dinosaurs had gone, the world must have seemed very empty. Gone were their huge bodies, the noise, mess and smell. But life carried on.

Many animals survived the KT mass extinction – insects, fishes, frogs, lizards, snakes, turtles, crocodiles, birds and mammals. The mammals in particular began to populate the world.

Ptilodus

Ptilodus came from a mammal group that had lived side-by-side with the dinosaurs, and which survived the mass extinction. It lived in trees, cutting and chewing its way through tough leaves and even wood.

The Palaeocene

The Palaeocene (65 to 56 mya) was the first time division of the Tertiary. No large animals survived. There were plants of many different sizes of course, but the surviving mammals and other creatures were all smaller than a cat. It took most of this epoch for life to diversify again.

Mammals

Mammals have hair, large brains, and they feed their young with milk. Mammals today include humans, monkeys, pigs, dogs, cats, mice, bats and whales. They have been successful because they can adapt to all habitats.

Chriacus

This 1m-long mammal probably fed on plants as well as insects and small mammals. It was one of the condylarths, raccoon-sized animals that included the ancestors of modern hoofed mammals, such as horses and cattle, but also of whales.

Plesiadapis

Primates are the large group of monkeys and apes. The oldest primates are Palaeocene forms such as *Plesiadapis*. This animal ran about in the trees, grasping the branches and using its long tail for balance as it leapt from tree to tree.

Cimolestes

Many unusual mammals survived from the Cretaceous, including the cimolestids, tree-dwellers that fed on insects with their pointed teeth. The cimolestids did not last long. However, they may be distantly related to some modern insect- or animal-eating mammals.

The Miocene and human origins

The Miocene was a key time in human evolution. In Africa, the great forests were filled with apes. By 15 mya, climates had become cooler and drier, and the forests smaller. Some apes, our ancestors, ventured out on the grassy plains and began to walk upright. The oldest human fossils are 6 million years old, and *Australopithecus* (below) lived 3–1 mya. Modern humans arose in Africa about 200,000 years ago.

Dinosaur facts

The world has changed a great deal since the dinosaurs disappeared. Most of the modern birds and mammals, including humans, came on the scene in the last 65 million years. Here are some major steps in evolution after the dinosaurs.

- **64 mya** Beginning of the Paleocene; the first primates – the order of mammals that includes monkeys, apes, and humans – appear.
- **60 mya** First rodents and bats appear.
- **55 mya** The first elephants, pigs, whales and songbirds appear.
- **40 mya** The first monkeys, and the first horses, cats and dogs appear.
- **35 mya** Grasses evolve from angiosperms and grassland spreads.
- **34 mya** Australia and South America separate from Antarctica; the first species of sabre-toothed cat, *Miomachairodus*, appears in Africa and Turkey.
- **35 mya** The largest land mammal ever appears – *Paraceratherium*, a giant rhinoceros of about 7.5m tall.
- **20 mya** First apes appear.
- **6 mya** The first in the human line, *Sahelanthropus* and *Orrorin*, appear in Africa.
- **4.8 mya** Mammoths appear in North America, Europe and Asia.
- **3 mya** South America re-joins North America at Panama, and their mammals mix.
- **2 mya** The first large-brained human, *Homo erectus*, appears in Africa.
- **1.8 mya** Beginning of the Pleistocene, the Great Ice Age with glacier ice spreading over a quarter of Earth's land surface; the woolly rhinoceros appears in Europe, North Africa and Asia.
- **1.4 mya** First fire-making by humans
- **150,000 years ago** The first members of our own species, *Homo sapiens*, appear in Africa.
- **100,000 years ago** The first modern humans appear in Asia and Europe.
- **32,000 years ago** Oldest known cave paintings are made in southern France.
- **18,000 years ago** Global warming begins, glacier ice begins to retreat and sea levels rise.
- **11,000 years ago** End of the Pleistocene and beginning of the Holocene (up to the present); the first humans appear in the Americas.

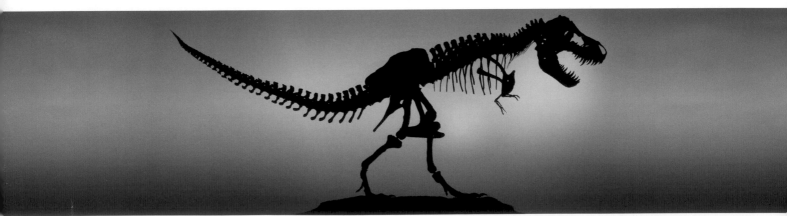

The fossil skeleton of a *Tyrannosaurus rex*, excavated in the Hell Creek Formation of South Dakota, USA

WEBSITES ON LIFE DURING THE MESOZOIC ERA

www.ucmp.berkeley.edu/mammal/mammal.html   An introduction to mammals.

www.ucmp.berkeley.edu/cenozoic/cenozoic.html   A guide to life over the last 65 million years.

www.bbc.co.uk/nature/life/Mammal/by/rank/all   A site that explores the life of mammals.

www.enchantedlearning.com/subjects/mammals/Evolution.shtml   All about early mammals.

Glossary

abelisaurid A large theropod, typically from South America.

adaptation The way in which an animal or plant changes over generations to suit a different environment.

ammonite A coiled, shelled sea creature, related to the modern octopus and squid.

anatomy The internal construction of an animal – the bones, muscles, sense organs and so on.

ancestor A relative from which an animal is descended.

ankylosaur A plant-eating, armoured dinosaur.

Archosauria The large group of animals that includes dinosaurs, crocodiles, birds and their ancestors.

Aves The Latin name for birds.

belemnite A sea creature with an internal shell, related to the modern cuttlefish.

biostratigraphy The use of fossils to date rocks.

bone plates Thickened scales of bone in, or sticking out of, the skin – usually for defence or fighting.

breeding Producing offspring.

camouflage The colour, markings or body shape that helps an animal to blend in with its background.

cannibal An animal that eats another of its own species.

Carboniferous The geological period (360–300 mya) when there were great coal forests, and the early amphibians and reptiles evolved.

Carnian The geological stage (218–216 mya) in the Late Triassic when dinosaurs evolved.

ceratopsian A plant-eating dinosaur with a horn on its head.

cimolestid A small, insect-eating mammal that lived from the Late Cretaceous onwards.

Coelurosauria A group of flesh-eating dinosaurs, many of them small.

compsognathid A small, flesh-eating dinosaur of the Late Jurassic and Early Cretaceous.

condylarth A group of Palaeocene mammals – some were plant-eaters and some were flesh-eaters.

confuciusornithid An early fossil bird from China.

conifer A tree with cones, such as a pine or spruce.

continental drift The movement of continents over millions of years.

crest A ridge or line of feathers on the head or down the back.

Cretaceous The geological period from 145–65 mya.

crocodilians Crocodiles and alligators and their ancestors.

cycad A tropical plant with fern-like fronds and large cones.

dicynodont A plant-eating, mammal-like reptile that lived during the Permian and Triassic.

digest To break down food in the body so that it can be absorbed.

Dinosauria The formal name for dinosaurs.

dromaeosaurid A small, flesh-eating dinosaur and a close relative of birds.

ecosystem A self-contained community of plants and animals and their environment, such as a desert.

evolution A gradual process of change in the genetic make-up of a species over generations.

extinction The dying out of a species.

extinction, mass The dying out of very many species at the same time.

fauna The animals that live together in a particular place.

fibres Tough tissues in plants.

formation Unit of rock of a particular age in a particular place.

fossil The ancient remains, trace or impression of an animal or plant, usually found in rocks.

geology The scientific study of rocks and minerals.

gingko A tree related to the conifer, such as the maidenhair tree of China.

global warming The warming of the air and sea on Earth, causing global climate change.

Gondwana The great prehistoric southern continent made up of what is now Africa, South America, Antarctica, Australia and India.

hadrosaur A plant-eating dinosaur with a bill similar to a duck's, often with a head crest.

herbivore A plant-eater.

ichthyosaur A marine reptile that looked like a shark or dolphin.

iguanodont A plant-eating dinosaur of the Early Cretaceous.

Jurassic The geological period from 200–245 mya.

KT Cretaceous–Tertiary (the letter 'K' is used because 'C' stands for Carboniferous).

Laurasia The great prehistoric northern continent made up of what is now North America, Europe and Asia.

magma Hot, melted rock deep under the Earth's crust.

mammal An animal with hair that produces milk for its young.

Maniraptora The group of flesh-eating dinosaurs that includes birds and their closest dinosaur relatives.

membrane A thin layer of tissue in an animal's body.

Mesozoic The geological era (251–65 mya) that includes the Triassic, Jurassic and Cretaceous.

meteorite A piece of rock or metal from space that may hit moons or planets such as the Earth.

migrate To move from one part of the world to another to find food or warm weather, or to produce young.

Miocene The geological period from 23–5 mya, when large mammals ruled the Earth.

Norian The geological stage of the Late Triassic (215–203 mya) when prosauropod dinosaurs lived.

Ornithischia The major dinosaur group that includes ornithopods, ceratopsians, ankylosaurs and stegosaurs.

ornithischian Describes a plant-eating dinosaur, a member of the Ornithischia.

ornithomimid An 'ostrich dinosaur', a flesh-eater with long neck and limbs.

ornithopod A two-legged, plant-eating dinosaur.

palaeontologist A scientist who studies fossils.

Paleocene The span of geological time from 65–56 mya, right after the extinction of the dinosaurs.

Pangaea The supercontinent during the Permian and Triassic periods.

plate tectonics The process deep in the Earth that drives the slow movements of the continents.

plesiosaur A long-necked, marine reptile that swam with broad paddles.

pliosaur A massive-headed, short-necked plesiosaur.

pollination The transfer of male cells to fertilize a female flower.

predator A meat-eater or hunter.

prey An animal that is hunted and eaten by another.

primate A monkey or ape.

prosauropod A long-necked ancestor of the sauropods that lived during the Late Triassic and Early Jurassic.

pterosaur A flying reptile that lived during the Jurassic and Cretaceous.

reptile A turtle, crocodile, lizard, snake or dinosaur.

rhynchosaur A Triassic plant-eater with a hooked snout.

Saurischia The major dinosaur group that includes the long-necked sauropodomorphs and the flesh-eating theropods.

sauropod A large, long-necked, plant-eating dinosaur.

sauropodomorphs The prosauropods and sauropods.

sediment Mud or sand that may turn into rock – mudstone and sandstone.

seed ferns Ancient plants that had leaves like ferns, but were sometimes as big as trees.

species A group of plants and animals that share characteristics.

specimen A fossil bone or skeleton.

spinosaur A large, flesh-eating dinosaur with a sail-like crest along its back.

stegosaur A plant-eating dinosaur with a row of plates down its back.

stratigraphy A branch of geology: the science of dating rocks.

teleost A typical bony fish, such as a salmon or a goldfish.

terrestrial Living on or in the ground on Earth.

Tertiary The geological period from 65–2 mya, after the dinsoaurs.

therizinosaur A bizarre, plant-eating theropod, from the Cretaceous, that had long, scythe-like fingers.

theropod A flesh-eating dinosaur.

Theropoda A group of flesh-eating dinosaurs.

titanosaur A giant sauropod, typical of the southern continents.

tree fern A primitive tree group with fern-like leaves.

Triassic The span of geological time from 251–200 mya.

troodontid A slender, flesh-eating

dinosaur closely related to birds.

tyrannosaur A large, flesh-eating dinosaur of the Cretaceous.

tyrannosaurid A member of the group containing tyrannosaurs and their relatives.

vertebrae The bones that make up the spinal column.

warm-blooded Having a constant body temperature, as in modern birds and mammals.

Index

Acknowledgements

The Publisher would like to thank the following for permission to reproduce their material. Every care has been taken to trace copyright holders.
Top = t; Bottom = b; Centre = c; Left = l; Right = r

Pages 11tr Universidad Federal of Rio do Sul, Brazil; 12lc Grupo Paleo, Argentina; 12lcb Corbis/Diego Goldberg/Sygma; 12lb Corbis/Louie Psihoyos; 13 Corbis/Hubert Stadler; 14bl with the Kind Permission of the Natural History Museum, London; 16tr Corbis/Louie Psihoyos; 17tcr Alamy/Kevin Schafer; 17br Shutterstock/psamtik; 20 Getty Images/DK; 21tr EvaK; 21cr Jens Lallensack; 22cl Natural History Museum, Stuttgart; 22–23t Natural History Museum, London; 22br Natural History Museum, Stuttgart; 23br Natural History Museum, London; 23br with thanks to Dr Mallison and his colleagues; 24b Natural History Museum, London; 25tr Corbis/Bettman; 29cr Dinosaur Project/University of Bristol; 29br Dinosaur Project/University of Bristol; 31tr with thanks to Doug Mercer; 31tr Science Photo Library/M-Sat Ltd; 31b Getty Images/Sigurgeir Jonasson/Nordic; 36tr Rob Gay/Dinodomain.com; 36–37 Shutterstock/Oscity; 37tl Shutterstock/Zack Frank; 37tr US Geological Society; 38tr Alamy/John Cancalosi; 38bl Courtesy of UC Museum of Palaeontology, Berkeley University; 38br Kobal/Amblin Universal; 41 Corbis/Louie Psihoyos; 43tc Mark Klinger/Carnegie Museum of Natural History; 43tr Mark Klinger/Carnegie Museum of Natural History; 43cr Institute of Vertebrate Palaeontology and Paleoanthropology, Beijing; 44b Dave Martill/ University of Portsmouth; 45t Getty Images/Matt Cardy; 47tl Natural History Museum, London; 47bc Science Photo Library/Michael Marten; 47br Science Photo Library/Sinclair Stammers; 49tl Geological Society; 49br Alamy/Tom Stack; 50tr Dept of Geology, Augustana College; 50b Dept of Geology, Augustana College; 52br iStock/leonello; 53tl Alamy/blinkwinkel; 53tr Alamy/Steve Bly; 53cr Natural History Museum, London; 53cr Natural History Museum, London; 57b Natural History Museum, London; 59tr Natural History Museum, London; 62tr With thanks to Roger Vaughan; 62br Corbis/Gaylon Wampler/Sygma; 63tr Science Photo Library/Philippe Plailly/Eurelios; 63bl Science Photo Library/Pascal Geotgheluck; 63br Science Photo Library/Philippe Plailly/Eurelios; 64 Corbis/Jonathan Blair; 66cl Corbis/Louie Psihoyos; 67 Mathew Wedel with the kind permission of the Museum of Natural History, Berlin; 72cl Alamy/North Wind Picture Agency; 72cr&b Corbis/Louie Psihoyos; 73cr Shutterstock/Francisco Javier Ballester Calonge; 75tr Ankyman; 76c EvaK; 78l Science Photo Library/Emily Rayfield; 78cr Emily Rayfield; 79 Getty Images/Iconica; 79br Corbis/Michael Yamashita; 83tl Corbis/Jonathan Blair; 83cr Corbis/Jonathan Blair; 83cl Natural History Museum, London; 85 Corbis/Louie Psihoyos; 86l Natural History Museum, London; 88l Ruth French with the kind permission of Mateus Octavio and the Museu da Lourinha, Portugal; 88bl Mateus Octavio/Museu da Lourinha; 89cl Mateus Octavio/Museu da Lourinha; 89bl Getty Images/AFP; 89br Reuters; 91cr Patrick Barth; 93cl Laikayiu; 94tr Natural History Museum, London; 94cl samwingkit; 94br Finblanco; 95 & 96 Corbis/Louie Psihoyos; 99tr Ray Bryant; 99tcl Natural History Museum, London; 99bcl Roy Shepherd at discoveringfossils.co.uk; 99br Natural History Museum, London; 100tr Natural History Museum, London; 100c Geological Society; 102l Science Photo Library/ George Bernard; 102tr Ray Bryant; 105br Natural History Museum, London; 106b Getty/NGS; 107 Professor Mike Benton; 108c David Dilcher and Sun Ge; 110c 86l Natural History Museum, London; 113 86l Natural History Museum, London; 114cl Getty/Spencer Platt; 115tr Getty/Frederic Brown; 116cl Dr Zhiou Zhonge; 117cr, 86l Natural History Museum, London; 119t, 86l Natural History Museum, London; 120cl Getty/DK; 120–121 Lou Maher; 121br Courtesy of Yale University; 124bl Natural History Museum, London; 125 Getty/AFP; 126tr Museum of Victoria, Australia; 127br Geological Society of Australia, Victoria Division; 130cl Getty/Topical Press Agency; 130cr Alamy/Marcus Wilson-Smith; 130b Getty/Hulton; 131cl Shutterstock/Dinoton; 131cr Corbis/Louie Psihoyos; 132cl Corbis/Louie Psihoyos; 132–133 Corbis/Louie Psihoyos; 133t Dean Steadman/Kingfisher; 134bl Gondwana Studios; 135br Gunnar Reiss; 137tr Corbis/Louie Psihoyos; 139 Natural History Museum, London; 139cr Photoshot; 140l Alamy/Bob Gibbons; 143tl Getty/Tim Boyle; 144l Sebastian Bergmann; 145r Natural History Museum, London; 146l Natural History Museum, London; 146c Andrew Farke and Lukas Panzarin; 147 Corbis/Louie Psihoyos; 149tl Dean Steadman/Kingfisher; 149br Dean Steadman/Kingfisher; 154 Corbis/Louie Psihoyos.

The publishers would like to thank the following artists: Julian Baker (26–27, 104b); Barry Croucher (Art Agency) (136–137); Peter Bull Agency (92c, 92bl, 93tl, 93tr, 93br, 102–10, 110tr, 110b, 111t, 111bl, 111br, 116tr, 116-117, 117tl, 117tr, 117cl); Ben Jones (34, 40l, 40c, 40br, 42l); Jane Pritchard/Linden Artists (82l); Roger Stewart (134–135, 135tl, 135tr); Sebastian Quigley (18r, 19tl, 30, 46, 76, 77, 84tl, 88br, 89tr, 98tr, 129, 131t, 131tr, 138l, 138cr, 138br, 139bl, 142cl, 150–151, 150b, 151); Stuart Jackson-Carter (Art Agency) (137cr, 137c, 137br, 137r, 140bl, 140–141, 141tr, 141b); Thomas Bayley (142b, 143tr, 143cr, 143r); all other illustrations by Steve and Sam Weston.